## Endorsements for *This Was CNN*

"Kent Heckenlively and Cary Poarch expose the dark underbelly of CNN, with the shocking truth that describes a fall from grace since the stellar days of the 1980s and 1990s and the abandonment of the noble goals espoused by founder Ted Turner. This book describes the death spiral of Turner's grand dream, caused by Jeff Zucker's violation of basic standards of journalism, shadowy relationships with intelligence agencies and an undeclared war on conservative politics. A must read."

—Max Swafford, Author, Editor

"This book may be about CNN, but its most shocking revelations have to do with the national security apparatus and its suffocating stranglehold on our government and our free press, through the use of social media companies and also through strategically embedded intelligence operatives."

—Ryan Hartwig, Facebook Whistleblower

"To state the obvious, CNN is far from the 'most trusted name in news.' That tag-line was adopted after the network's meteoric rise in the 1980s as the go-to network for on-the-spot reporting of breaking news and programming featuring lively debates from differing points of view. What happened? How did it become one of the least trusted names in news? Finally, we can learn the answer. It is all here in *This Was CNN*. Everyone interested in understanding the demise of mainstream American media as sources of truth should read it."

—Dennis Prager is the co-founder of Prager University, a nationally syndicated radio talk show host and author of ten bestselling books, including most recently, the third of his five-volume commentary on the first five books of the Bible, *The Rational Bible*.

"Heckenlively and Poarch do a deep dive into the cable news giant, revealing an obvious and hysterical bias against conservatives, and the nightmare possibilities of mounting cyber warfare and control by our intelligence agencies. An important book!"

–Eric Metaxas, #1 *New York Times* bestselling author and nationally syndicated radio host

"Heckenlively and Poarch do a deep dive into the cable news giant, revealing not just the bias against conservatives, but the terrifying possibility that they are preparing cyber warfare against their enemies, as well as being controlled by our intelligence agencies. Maybe we've been getting it wrong by calling it "fake news." Maybe we should be calling it "spook news."

—Zach Vorhies, Google whistleblower, author, and Founder of Blastvideo.com

# THIS ~~IS~~ WAS
# CNN

## HOW SEX, LIES, AND SPIES UNDID
## THE WORLD'S WORST NEWS NETWORK

Kent Heckenlively
*and* Cary Poarch

BOMBARDIER
BOOKS

Published by Bombardier Books
An Imprint of Post Hill Press
ISBN: 978-1-63758-626-6
ISBN (eBook): 978-1-63758-627-3

This Was CNN:
How Sex, Lies, and Spies Undid the World's Worst News Network
© 2022 by Kent Heckenlively and Cary Poarch
All Rights Reserved

Cover Design by Matt Margolis

Post Hill Press
New York • Nashville
posthillpress.com

Published in the United States of America
1 2 3 4 5 6 7 8 9 10

To those who hunger for objective, non-biased information.

To act upon one's convictions while others wait, to create a positive force in a world where cynics abound, to provide information to people when it wasn't available before, to offer those who want it, a choice. For the American people, whose thirst for understanding and a better life have made this venture possible, for the cable industry, whose pioneering spirit caused this great step forward in communications, and for those employees of Turner Broadcasting, whose total commitment to their company has brought us together today, I dedicate the news channel for America, the Cable News Network.

—CNN founder, Ted Turner, on the network's first broadcast, June 1, 1980[1]

# CONTENTS

It was Daniel Ellsberg who once said that to be a whistleblower is to step outside the Great Chain of Being—not join another religion, but to enter outer space.

Whistleblowers who come to Project Veritas are no longer part of the organization they came from, nor are they employees of the news organization they present their findings to.

They are akin to space walking astronauts who bravely cut their umbilical cord from the mother ship.

To be brave. To do something. To be the answer to the age-old question, "What can I do to make a difference?"

In our country, to follow your conscience when many are told to sit down or forced to shut up requires an extreme amount of nerve, craziness, or courage. Maybe a bit of all three. It also requires a firmness of constitution and strong centered morality in a world where the center cannot hold.

I met Cary in February 2019, while he was covering the Conservative Political Action Conference (CPAC) in Washington, D.C. for CNN at the time. He approached me while I was signing books to tell me he worked for a "3-letter" organization. At first, I thought he meant a federal agency—but would later find out he worked for CNN. He was inspired by something another brave whistleblower had done at Facebook. She had leaked internal documents within Facebook showing they were "de-boosting" commentary from conservatives on the platform—like Steven Crowder, for example.

From that moment up until October 2019, when the #ExposeCNN series was launched, Cary worked tirelessly to uncover what was happening within the network—at huge risk for his job, his family, as well as his mental health. Keep in mind that Cary had a baby on the way during this period—which added to his daily workload and stress. I recall Cary struggled with the ethics of recording a colleague at CNN—Patrick Davis—because Patrick was a good guy trapped in a bad environment. "I hate what we've become. We could be so much better than we are," said the Field Operations Manager who worked at the network for twenty-five years. That moment—and Cary's decision to capture it—became a staple of the Project Veritas curriculum. The public's right to know what the Field Operations Manager, Patrick Davis, said ultimately won out in the end.

As Cary said in his interview to me, it wasn't that he betrayed CNN, it was that CNN betrayed their vital mission of being the most trusted name in news. Cary strapped on that undercover camera because of his employer's betrayal and served We The People.

Courage is not the absence of fear. It is the presence of fear and the will to overcome it.

Cary's courage led to video recordings that exposed then-CNN president Jeff Zucker's "personal vendetta" against Trump, the corporate model that encourages click-bait and rating-driven journalism instead of truth telling, as well as the wide-ranging partisanship of many employees at the cable network. The four videos that were launched obtained millions of views and were widely covered by all sides of the media.

Courageous people coming out follows courageous people taking action. Cary's efforts inspired the ABC News Insider who leaked the bombshell Amy Robach tape—where the ABC anchor admitted she buried the Epstein story for three years to appease the Clintons and the British Royal Family.

Since his work with Project Veritas, Cary has flourished. He continues to devote himself to the truth and to America. He is an example to be followed.

I speak for everyone at Project Veritas when I say that Cary is admired and appreciated for everything he has done and everything he embodies. I can only hope that there are more people like Cary out there.

When you read this book, keep all of this in mind. But also remember that Project Veritas is constantly looking for the next Cary Poarch-style Insider.

It is up to all of us to Be Brave and Do Something. Cary did his part—others must follow in his footsteps. The media, our country, and frankly the world is a better place for what Cary has done in following his conscience. I encourage others out there to follow his example.

**James O'Keefe III**

# How We've Become Unbalanced

On the Wednesday morning after Donald Trump beat Hillary Clinton in the presidential election in November 2016, I was sitting in a science department meeting for the middle school at which I teach, when our principal, Sharon (pseudonym), came into the room.

Sharon was about my age, mid-fifties, short blond hair, a runner like my wife, open about being lesbian, and wanted people to think of her as something of an Ellen DeGeneres type—charming, funny, hospitable, and not strident in her beliefs at all. In fact, Sharon even had a moment of brief national celebrity when NBC News came to our school to shoot a segment about her quirky habit of playing music on a boom box and dancing in her orange safety vest at the crosswalk to welcome students in the morning as they scurried to their first class. It was one of those short, uplifting vignettes in which the audience was supposed to think, *Wow, I wish I had a middle school principal like that!*

Sharon walked into the room on the morning after Trump's election, looked at all of us, put her hands on her hips, and said, "Well, fuck! Who needs a hug?"

Even after my years in public education in California I was stunned by this vulgar comment. I'm sure she thought we were cool enough to accept the lingo and that, of course, we agreed with her. But not everyone did. My colleagues laughed, a few of them took her up on the hug offer, but I just sat there, puzzled by how to respond.

How had such an enormous gap developed between the way I'd been taught to handle political differences in my youth and the reality I was living as an adult? As a public-school teacher, I'm aware of the enormous influence I have on young minds and of the professional demeanor I try to maintain with my colleagues. I don't think it's my place to be political as a science teacher or to be so dismissive of half the adult population who voted for Donald Trump.

When the presidential elections roll around every four years, my students will inevitably ask, "Who are you voting for, Mr. Heckenlively? The Democrats or the Republicans?"

I always respond with something along the lines of, "I think the Republicans have some good things to say, and so do the Democrats."

For most of them it's enough, while others will continue to engage me, saying things, such as, "I know you're a Democrat because you're a teacher," or "I know you're a Republican because you always dress so nicely in slacks and a jacket."

I only smile enigmatically.

I'm a sphinx about sharing my political beliefs at school. The parents of my students are Republicans and Democrats. The only thing I want my students to remember about me is the science I taught them, and hopefully how I often had more faith in them than they did in themselves.

I grew up in a house with a dark-haired, olive-skinned Sicilian mother and a blond-haired, blue-eyed Swedish-German father. They met at the 1956 Republican Convention in San Francisco, so I'm guessing you might see their influence on my politics. My parents were both well-educated and enjoyed talking politics, but even more than that they enjoyed interesting people. When one of my father's friends turned out to be close to local political figures like Senators Barbara

Boxer and Diane Feinstein, and Representative Nancy Pelosi, my parents jumped at the chance to go to events these politicians attended. They were curious and willing to listen to different points of view.

Now you understand my programming. I believe that Americans can calmly discuss *anything*. And when Americans speak honestly to each other, hopefully both sides learn something they didn't fully comprehend before.

I should also note that, from the time that the Cable News Network (CNN) was launched, on June 1, 1980, the network had no more devoted fan than my mother. As long as somebody was awake at our house, it was a good bet that CNN was on the television. CNN anchor Bernard Shaw and talk show host Larry King were the two people in this world my parents respected the most. For a scrapbook from my teenage years, I even cut out an advertisement featuring billionaire bad boy CNN founder, Ted Turner, at the helm of his yacht, *Courageous*, as an example of the kind of successful, colorful man I hoped to become one day.

I've lived in California all my life, so I'm aware of the liberal drift from the days of Ronald Reagan to current governor Gavin Newsom. Yet, I still believed that there are lines that one should not cross, and my principal had stepped egregiously over them.

And yet, it wasn't the first time she'd failed to uphold standards that had once been norms and were still displayed on signs throughout the halls of our school, such as the Apple slogan to "Think Different" along with pictures of people like musician Miles Davis, Nobel Prize winner Nelson Mandela, and famed aviatrix Amelia Earhart.

In 2014 I'd cowritten a book called *Plague: One Scientist's Intrepid Search for the Truth about Human Retroviruses and Chronic Fatigue Syndrome (ME/CFS), Autism, and Other Diseases* with twenty-year government scientist Dr. Judy Mikovits, which raised the possibility that myalgic encephalomyelitis/chronic fatigue syndrome (ME/CFS), a puzzling epidemic that struck down mainly women in the 1980s in concert with the HIV/AIDS epidemic, was caused by a mouse virus that had crossed into the human population via vaccines that were grown in mouse tissue. (There also appeared to be a connection between this virus and autism, which greatly interested me as my daughter suffers from this condition.) For those who have worried about mercury or aluminum salts in vaccines, this raised a new area of inquiry, about whether it was ever a good idea to grow human viruses in animal tissues, as other viruses from those animals might hitch a ride back in the resulting vaccine.

At the time, I'd sensed an enormous amount of hostility from my fellow science teachers (none of whom currently work with me), and it required me to have a talk with my principal. I told her of my concerns, and she asked what she could do.

On the outside of each of our classrooms and the administrative offices is a small placard where we list what we're currently reading, broadcasting to the students our belief in lifelong learning. I said, "You could put up that you're reading my book. I think it's quite an accomplishment for one of your teachers to publish a book. You should be celebrating it."

"But I don't know if I believe what you wrote," she replied.

"You haven't read what I wrote, so you really have no idea what I believe," I pointed out. "Besides, I didn't think we encouraged people to read only things they already believed. I thought we wanted people to read things which might occasionally challenge their beliefs."

My argument went nowhere, she never put on her placard that she was reading my book, and I had to endure being ostracized by a few insufferable science teachers until they finally chose to leave a couple years later.

So much for the idea that she supported people who might "Think Different."

\*\*\*

The point of my story is that those types of violations of political norms were seen throughout our culture. They seemed to permeate so much of American life in ways that were alien to American traditions.

I belong to a book club at a nearby bookstore, and there were generally about fifteen to twenty participants, a lively and eclectic group of people, mostly ten to twenty years older than me. A few months into 2017, one of the group, a former writer for the *San Jose Mercury News*, declared that she had unfriended on Facebook any of her friends or family who had voted for Donald Trump. In addition, she said she was going to work very hard in 2020 to ensure that Trump was defeated, unless he'd already been impeached by that time.

I wondered, *How are you going to convince people to vote for Trump's opponent, if you won't talk to the people who voted for him the first time?*

Of course, I kept such thoughts to myself, as I figured if I voiced even the slightest opposition to her ideas, I would quickly find myself on the same side as her out-of-favor friends and family.

*\*\*\**

In April 2020, just a few weeks into the nationwide COVID-19 lockdown, I wrote my second book with Judy Mikovits, *Plague of Corruption: Restoring Faith in the Promise of Science*, and it became the runaway science bestseller of 2020, reaching the top spot of all books on Amazon for a week, and spending six weeks on the *New York Times* bestseller list.

Because of this success, I was fortunate enough to meet Zach Vorhies, better known to the public as the "Google whistleblower," who took more than 950 pages of internal documents demonstrating the company's political bias and turned them over to the US Justice Department and Project Veritas. Zach and I wrote a book called, *Google Leaks: A Whistleblower's Exposé of Big Tech Censorship*, which was published in early August 2021.

As a result of meeting Zach, I was introduced to another whistleblower, Ryan Hartwig, who had documented political bias in content moderation at Facebook. He had a manuscript that needed some assistance, and our resulting book, *Behind the Mask of Facebook: A*

*Whistleblower's Shocking Story of Big Tech Bias and Censorship*, was published in mid-August 2021. At the end of August, my third book with Judy Mikovits, *Ending Plague: A Scholar's Obligation in an Age of Corruption*, came out. I'd been very busy.

In late July 2021, Zach Vorhies invited me to FreedomFest in Rapid City, South Dakota, to meet the Project Veritas team. At the group's booth in the exhibition hall, I met several of the members, and Zach pointed out Cary Poarch, the CNN whistleblower, a name I already knew.

I walked up to him, stuck out a hand, and said, "Cary, I want to thank you for endorsing my book."

He gave me a curious look, as if to say, *When the hell did I do that?* I let him squirm for a moment, then said, "You gave a very nice endorsement to my book with Ryan Hartwig, the Facebook whistleblower."

"Oh, you're the author," he replied. "Say, listen, I want to talk to you about the book I want to write."

In my mind I thought, *Big pharma, Google, Facebook. Of course, CNN should be next on the list.* It seemed I was finding a new career as the unofficial biographer for the Project Veritas whistleblowers.

"Give me a month or so to catch my breath," I said, "then let's start in September."

It was great fun to hang around with the Project Veritas team and Cary. James O'Keefe had several of his whistleblowers at the conference, and they put on a forty-five-minute stage show that was part lecture, rock concert, and pep rally. I was mesmerized.

O'Keefe is such a celebrity that it's a challenge when he wants to take his large traveling crew and assorted friends to dinner. With Zach and Cary lending me the necessary street cred, I was traveling with the Project Veritas posse in about six white vans, each seating about ten people, on our way to dinner.

I rode shotgun in the lead van as we drove to a nearby restaurant that was supposed to be closed. But when Project Veritas called up and asked if they could have, essentially, a private party, the restaurant quickly agreed. When we arrived, the owner, a woman who looked to be in her early thirties, opened the door and in a breathless voice said, "Oh my God, Project Veritas! I didn't believe it was really you! I love you guys!"

There were curtains on the windows so nobody could see us as we dined, and I felt like I was traveling with a modern-day outlaw gang, the kind the authorities hate and the local population sees as heroes. Dinner lasted for several hours; then as the restaurant was closing at about nine thirty somebody said, "Hey, there's a party at some guy's house in the Black Hills, about thirty minutes away from here."

I joined the Project Veritas caravan to "some guy's house" in the Black Hills, and around midnight (we got lost several times) we were at the house. It had a lovely outdoor area, wooded, and was right next to a rushing stream beneath a carpet of the blackest night and the brightest stars. And of course, I asked myself, *What the hell am I doing here? I should be back at the hotel. My flight leaves early tomorrow.*

But then I inhaled, smelling the pines, hearing the sound of the stream, seeing the friendly lights from the house, the people sitting around talking about important things, and thought, *No, being here tonight is worth missing a couple hours of sleep.*

I've been incredibly lucky, writing first with Judy Mikovits, then diving into Big Tech stories about Google and Facebook, and now working with Cary Poarch on this book about CNN. I like to think I write stories about heroes, people who put themselves at enormous risk because they believe there is something the public has a right to know.

When one of my books is a success, like my books with Dr. Mikovits, it seems as if suddenly the whole world is talking about them. My wife jokes that it seems as if people only see the first name on the book and not the second, the position I usually take. When I complain about it, she brings me back to Earth by saying, "You're probably safer that way."

I may not get the credit for my part of the process, but I have the honor of telling the tales of heroes. There is so much negativity in today's culture, and these books do not shy away from describing what is wrong in many of our institutions. However, at their heart, these are also stories of exceptional courage and integrity. I believe they have the potential to rebalance our political discussions, our society, and, perhaps, the way we treat each other.

I have added Cary Poarch to my personal pantheon of heroes.

# The Vision of Captain Outrageous

He was nicknamed "Captain Outrageous" and the "Mouth of the South"[2]—media mogul and buccaneer billionaire Ted Turner, a flamboyant, outsize personality who dominated the American imagination from the late 1970s to the mid-1990s—culminating in his being named *Time* magazine's Man of the Year in 1991. Turner stood six-foot-one, was trim, and sported a thin mustache like Clark Gable in *Gone with the Wind*, a movie he would later come to own through the purchase of the MGM movie library and show often on his Turner Network Television channel.

If you paid attention during those days, you couldn't help but follow Ted Turner's exploits, not knowing whether his latest daring venture would be a smashing success or crushing defeat. Ted always gave good entertainment value. The opening paragraph of the 1991 *Time* article about Turner captured the duality of this troubled visionary:

> Ted Turner's life may best be understood as a startling series of narrowly missed disasters. When he skippered his yacht in Britain's prestigious Fastnet race in 1979, he was so absorbed in victory that he did not

even know a gale was killing 15 yachtsmen in the boats behind him. His costly acquisition of MGM's movie library in 1986, widely considered a bonehead move at the time, now looks like a bargain the Japanese would envy. The Atlanta Braves, which Turner bought in 1976, snuffled along in the gutter for years, then went from last place to first in their division this year and lost the World Series by only a bat's whoosh. And CNN, once derided as the "Chicken Noodle Network" for its low wages and amateurish presentation, is now the video medium of record.[3]

Turner was bold and brash, excellent copy for the newspapers, and yet there was a remarkably sad story behind him, of a father he idolized, but also of a father who brutalized him. Sometimes the father would beat him with a wire coat hanger, and at other times, if his disappointment with Ted was severe, his father would turn the tables and tell his son to beat him.

"He laid down on the bed and gave me a razor strap and he said, 'Hit me harder,'" Turner told interviewer David Frost. "And that hurt me more than getting the beating myself. I couldn't do it. I just broke down and cried." The most famous story of this dynastic war is the time Ed Turner sent Ted a letter at Brown University for having chosen to study the Greek classics. "I almost puked on the way home today...I think you are rapidly becoming a jackass and the sooner you get out of that filthy atmosphere, the better it will suit me," Ed Turner wrote. The angry son retaliated cunningly: he published the letter in the college newspaper. But he eventually switched his major to economics.[4]

There is much in Turner's story to make one wonder how he ever made anything out of his life, much less become one of the great historical figures in media. At the age of six, Ted was sent away to boarding school; in the fifth grade, he was sent to a military academy, and his father "punished him at home for such omissions as failing to read a new book every two days and charged him rent during summer vacations."[5]

At the age of fifty-three, Ed Turner shot himself, and Ted went to work saving the family billboard business, which his father had left on the edge of collapse. After rescuing the company, he set his sights on loftier goals, hoping to exorcise the wound of his father's disapproval.

> Turner proved far more adept even than his father at the billboard business. So as the money rolled in, he turned to sailing and broadcasting in pursuit of his father's elusive benediction. By 1982, when he was 43, he had successfully defended the America's Cup, launched the first station distributed nationally to cable systems via satellite and the first 24-hour news network, and made the first edition of the Forbes 400 list—enough success, he says, to have begun to lay "the ghost" of that paternal judgment "to rest." But he was still an emotional cripple. Turner's role model as a grownup remained an alcoholic father whose behavior was as extreme as it was unpredictable, who boasted about his sexual conquests, fought often with his wife and ultimately divorced her after 20 years.[6]

The picture painted of Ted's father was of a predatory capitalist who was never satisfied with personal relationships and viewed people as commodities to be whipped into shape, and if that didn't work out, they were sold at a loss. While Ted may have clashed with his father, he emulated much of his negative personal behavior.

He was such a determined womanizer that he made clear to Janie before their marriage in 1964 that he had no intention of becoming monogamous, according to several intimates. "I didn't like being alone on the road" is how Turner today explains his numerous entanglements. Robert Wussler, his former senior executive vice president, says Turner's amorous philosophy was "a port in every storm." In some cases, it was literally a woman in every port: he once scandalized the yachting circuit by sailing around with a blonde Frenchwoman tending galley, sometimes topless.[7]

By virtue of his upbringing, Ted was clearly a damaged human being, and yet he achieved remarkable things. His style was to find an opening in some untapped area created by technological change, talk a lot about how he was going to succeed, then do it. One of his favorite slogans was "Early to bed, early to rise, work like hell and advertise!"[8] His bluster and bravado were as much a part of his marketing strategy as his financial statements.

And yet, it had all paid off for Turner by 1991, including putting to rest some of his personal demons.

> Among the events carried live by CNN in 1991 were the Baghdad bombings that began the Persian Gulf War, the Soviet coup and the emergence of Russian President Boris N. Yeltsin, the trial and acquittal of William Kennedy Smith and the confirmation hearings of Supreme Court Justice Clarence Thomas.

> The honor caps a busy year for Turner. The television magnate's Atlanta Braves won the National League pennant before losing a dramatic seven-game World

Series to the Minnesota Twins, and he married actress
Jane Fonda earlier this month.[9]

Ted Turner seemed to be a classic American character, part visionary, part huckster, taking on the establishment, and when he started
winning, changed from a Peter Pan–like man-child into somebody
responsible, not just worried about profit, fame, or the next woman in
port. From the 1991 *Time* piece on Turner:

> For the past six years, Turner has made a public
> career of saving the planet…. He used to talk about
> war as an efficient way to weed out the weak mem-
> bers of society; in 1986 to promote world peace, he
> staged the Goodwill Games in Moscow, on which
> he lost $26 million, and staged them again last year
> in Seattle, losing an additional $44 million…. "If we
> don't make the right choice after we have all the infor-
> mation, then we don't deserve to live," he told mem-
> bers of People for the American Way, a liberal organi-
> zation that awarded him its Spirit of Liberty prize in
> November. "I don't think that's the case, but it's going
> to be real close."[10]

Turner had evolved into somebody who wanted to keep the
United States and the Soviet Union from getting into a nuclear war
that would devastate the planet, as well as promote environmental-
ism. For a time, he was the largest landowner in the United States and
currently runs more than forty-five thousand head of buffalo at his
various ranches,[11] trying to restore that magnificent animal to some
of its historic range.

While there were many personal episodes that led him to the
brink of personal change, it seems to have been the psychiatric medi-
cation lithium, prescribed by Frank Pittman, MD, that brought about
the greatest change in Turner.

Pittman did two important things for Turner. The first was to put him on the drug lithium, which is generally used to treat manic depression as well as a milder tendency toward mood swings known as cyclothymic personality. Turner's colleagues and J.J. Ebaugh, the woman for whom he left Janie, suddenly saw an enormous change in his behavior. "Before it was pretty scary to be around the guy sometimes because you never knew what in the world was going to happen next. If he was about to fly off the handle, you just never knew. That's why the whole world was on pins and needle around him," says Ebaugh, "but with lithium he became very even tempered. Ted's just one of those miracle cases. I mean, lithium is great stuff, but in Ted's particular case, lithium is a miracle."[12]

The second important thing Dr. Pittman did for Turner was to get him to explore his relationship with his father and put those demons to rest. What remained of Turner still had the same fire and outrageousness, but the edges had been smoothed. His marriage to Jane Fonda would end in 2001, but it seemed the young rebel was on his way to becoming an elder statesman.

By 2003, however, Turner had been maneuvered out of CNN, as detailed in *60 Minutes* with Mike Wallace:

He's in charge of just about nothing. He doesn't even have a voice any more in the running of his baby, Cable News Network [CNN]. He says his formal role has been that of advisor—but it's not really what he wants to be.

When the plan to merge Time-Warner with AOL was first announced, Turner voted for it with unbridled joy.

At the time, he said he "did it with as much or more excitement and enthusiasm as on the night I first made love 42 years ago."

But now he has a different view: "Well, you know, on the eve of something like that, it was very clear that it was going to go through. So I might as well have gone along with it."

Was it a big mistake? "It was," says Turner. "Absolutely."[13]

What becomes of rebels, renegades, and revolutionaries as they get older? Do they create genuinely different ways of doing things, a new and better kingdom? Or does their rebellion eventually become co-opted, a high price offered for the rebel's remarkable creation, along with promises it will be well-treated, only for the rebel to later realize these were false promises?

When CNN was launched in June 1980 in Atlanta, Turner said he hoped that its coverage would "bring together in brotherhood and kindness and friendship and in peace the people of this nation and this world."[14]

Ted Turner has great wealth, but since the deal in 2003 he has had little influence on the public dialog as it has degraded to the point where many barely even recognize it. I am certain that many younger readers of this book will not even know the name Ted Turner.

But they do know his creation, CNN.

In the pages of this book, Kent Heckenlively and I ask how far CNN has strayed from the vision of its founder.

# CHAPTER ONE

# Two Years at CNN Is Barely Enough to Scratch the Surface

Cary spent a little more than two years at CNN, working as a satellite uplink technician under contract, at the Washington, DC, bureau. He had amazing access. He was no more than thirty yards away from the desk of long-time CNN anchor Wolf Blitzer. He might bump into some of the other anchors or reporters, like Jake Tapper or Dana Bash, walking down the hallway or see chief legal analyst Jeffrey Toobin eating alone by himself again in the CNN cafeteria. Cary even got to listen in on CNN president Jeff Zucker's daily 9 a.m. calls in which he gave direction to his news and production team about what they should cover that day.

For about six of those months, Cary was an undercover operative for Project Veritas, filming his interactions and uncovering what he believed to be the most important story in the world, the rampant political bias at CNN, which billed itself as "the most trusted name in news."

When his video for Project Veritas was released on October 14, 2019, as well as several that followed, he thought he'd told the story.

After all, everybody was calling him the "CNN whistleblower." Hadn't he spilled all the secrets?

He still believes that he added important pieces of information to the public debate, especially concerning political bias at the network. He'd remain preoccupied with the CNN story, assisting the production of several subsequent stories about CNN by Project Veritas, where he now works as an investigative journalist.

However, as the investigations for this book will clearly show, he had barely scratched the surface.

\*\*\*

If you can believe it, Cary started his work for CNN in the summer of 2017 as a die-hard Bernie Sanders supporter, having spent much of the previous year volunteering at least ten hours a week for his campaign in Colorado, where Cary lived at that time. Like many Bernie Sanders supporters, he was stunned when Bernie essentially threw in the towel in favor of Hillary Clinton in March 2017. Along with many of his fellow disillusioned Bernie Bros, he wondered if Bernie's wife had been taken hostage or whether their favorite democratic socialist had received a really big payout.

The CNN bureau in Washington is physically located in the top four floors of an eleven-story building on First Street, not far from Union Station. Cary's job at CNN was to make sure that its two satellite trucks were ready to go at a moment's notice, drive the vehicle to the location, get all the technology working to support the reporter or anchor in the field, and when the story was over, pack up all the gear and drive the truck back to the Washington bureau.

Cary is a social creature by nature, so with the abundant free time offered by the job, he'd roam through the CNN office, introducing himself and making general conversation. Cary is originally from the South and knows how to be cordial, so when he saw somebody, he'd stick out his hand and say, "Hi, I'm Cary Poarch, the new engineer. I'll be in charge of the satellite trucks." His impression of most of the people was that they were friendly, forthcoming, and very professional.

Early in the job he introduced himself to Wolf Blitzer, and they had a friendly conversation. Everybody loved Wolf Blitzer.

Cary got a totally different reaction from anchor Jake Tapper, who seemed surprised that a lowly employee would speak to him and sputtered out a quick "Hi!" before retreating to his office. Cary remembers thinking, *I guess it takes all kinds.*

Chief political correspondent and anchor Dana Bash and chief national correspondent John King were always friendly and good conversationalists.

Over time, his favorite person at CNN became legal analyst Evan Perez. He was genuinely courteous, respectful, and always willing to share his legal opinions. Evan relished getting into hypothetical conversations about where a developing news story might go and didn't mind sharing his opinions about people like Attorney General Bill Barr or what he thought might be contained in the upcoming Mueller Report—which people at CNN were awaiting with the anticipation one imagines the ancient Israelites had for Moses as he descended from Mount Sinai with the Ten Commandments.

\*\*\*

Cary's disillusionment with CNN began with the Charlottesville riots of August 11 and 12, 2017. For months there had been simmering tension over the question of whether it was appropriate to have statues of Confederate figures in public parks, as were still found in the South.

As a Southerner himself, Cary has mixed feelings about this question and genuinely appreciates the opinions on both sides. If you put a gun to his head and force him to take a side, he'll tell you, "Let's take them down." But he also understands that those who want them to remain are not necessarily racists. Just because somebody chose the wrong side doesn't mean he is devoid of any humanity or goodness.

On the night before the planned August 12, 2017, protest, there was a preliminary gathering, which looked to many as if the demons of America's past had been resurrected. As later reported:

> In the evening, hundreds of white nationalists gather at University of Virginia ahead of August 12th's planned Unite the Right rally. Wielding torches, their chants include phrases such as "white lives matter," "Jews will not replace us," and the Nazi-associated phrase "blood and soil."[15]

Like most in the country, Cary was following these reports with horror. When he went to sleep on August 11, he had a sneaking suspicion that this would be the first time he'd be driving the CNN satellite truck to a location to cover a breaking story.

Shortly after 10:30 a.m. on August 12, he got the call to take the truck down to Charlottesville, Virginia, and within an hour he was on his way. The CNN engineer who would handle the tech after he set it up was in the passenger seat on his laptop, providing updates on the spiraling violence. As later described by FactCheck.org:

> **1:02 p.m.**—Corinne Geller, a spokesman for Virginia State Police, says in an interview with Fox News that "all sides" had engaged in throwing bottles and other debris in what had been—as of that point—a violent, but non-fatal confrontation.
>
> **1:19 p.m.**—Trump tweets, "We ALL must be united and condemn all that hate stands for. There is no place for this kind of violence in America. Let us come together as one!"
>
> **1:31 p.m.**—CNN airs an interview with [David] Duke at the rally, which he said represents a "turning point." The former Klan grand wizard said, "We're going to fulfill the promises of Donald Trump. That's what we believed in. That's why we voted for Donald Trump, because he said we're going to take our country back. And that's what we gotta do."

**1:40 p.m.**—A driver, later identified as James Alex Fields, Jr., speeds down Fourth Street and into a crowd of counter-protestors who are marching in the street. Fields then throws the car in reverse and speeds away.

**2:01 p.m.**—On Twitter, Duke criticizes Trump's tweet calling for everyone to "condemn all that hate stands for." Duke retweets Trump's post and writes, "So, after decades of White Americans being targeted for discriminated & anti-White hatred, we come together as a people, and you attack us?"[16]

Why was CNN airing an interview with David Duke if it was interested in lowering the potential for violence? It seemed as if CNN was fanning the flames of violence and blaming it on President Trump.

However, an hour and twenty-three minutes after the car attack by James Alex Fields Jr., and three minutes after the death of Heather Heyer was announced, Trump delivered remarks about the ongoing violence. Here is part of what he said:

> But we're closely following the terrible events unfolding in Charlottesville, Virginia. We condemn in the strongest possible terms this egregious display of hatred, bigotry, and violence, on many sides. On many sides. It's been going on for a long time in our country. Not Donald Trump, not Barack Obama. This has been going on for a long, long time.

> It has no place in America. What is vital now is a swift restoration of law and order and the protection of innocent lives. No citizen should ever fear for their safety and security in our society, and no child should ever be afraid to go outside and play or be with their parents and have a good time.

I just got off the phone with the Governor of Virginia, Terry McAuliffe, and we agreed that the hate and the division must stop right now. We have to come together as Americans with love for our Nation and true affection—really, and I say this so strongly—true affection for each other.[17]

Carey was not a Trump supporter at this time, but he did believe in basic fairness. And Trump had said what he expected any president to say in response to a tragic event.

A few days after the attack, Cary and the engineer went to the house of Marcus Martin, a black man who had been injured in the car attack. They patched him into an interview with Chris Cuomo, in which Martin said he'd simply gone to the rally to oppose the racists and promote love.[18] It was powerful to be in the room with this man as he spoke about what he'd endured.

On Monday, August 14, 2017, less than forty-eight hours after the car attack, Trump spoke again about the Charlottesville violence. This is part of what he said:

I just met with FBI Director Christopher Wray and Attorney General Jeff Sessions. The Department of Justice has opened a civil rights investigation into the deadly car attack that killed one innocent American and wounded 20 others. To anyone who acted criminally in this weekend's racist violence, you will be held fully accountable. Justice will be delivered.

As I said on Saturday, we condemn in the strongest possible terms this egregious display of hatred, bigotry, and violence. It has no place in America. And as I have said many times before, no matter the color of our skin, we all live under the same laws, we salute the same great flag, and we are all made by the same almighty God. We must love each other, show affection for each other, and unite together in condemnation of hatred, bigotry, and violence. We must rediscover the bonds of love and loyalty that bring us together as Americans.

Racism is evil. And those who cause violence in its name are criminals and thugs, including the KKK, neo-Nazis, white supremacists, and other hate groups that are repugnant to everything we hold dear as Americans. We are a nation founded on the truth that all of us are created equal. We are equal in the eyes of our Creator. We are equal under the law. And we are equal under the Constitution. Those who spread violence in the name of bigotry strike at the very core of America.[19]

From Cary's perspective, the media, especially CNN, was creating a narrative in which Trump was responsible for the violence.

Then on August 15, 2017, came the exchange that would launch CNN into its "fine people" hoax, which would follow Trump throughout his presidency. Here is part of that exchange:

REPORTER: You said there was hatred, there was violence on both sides?

TRUMP: Well, I do think there's blame. Yes. I think there is blame on both sides. You look at both sides. I think there is blame on both sides. And I have no doubt about it. And you don't have doubt about it, either. And if you reported it accurately, you would say—

REPORTER [Cuts off the President]:—The neo-Nazis started this thing. They showed up in Charlottesville to protest—

TRUMP: Excuse me. They didn't put themselves down as neo-Nazis. And you had some very bad people in that group. But you also had people that were very fine people on both sides.

You had people in that group—excuse me, excuse me—I saw the same pictures as you did. You had people in that group that were there to protest the taking down of, to them, a very, very important statue and the renaming of a park from Robert E. Lee to another name—

[Cross-talk]

TRUMP: George Washington was a slave owner. Was George Washington a slave owner? So, will George Washington now lose his status? Are we going to take down—excuse me—are we going to take down statues to George Washington? How about Thomas Jefferson? What do you think of Thomas Jefferson? You like him? [Reporter apparently nods.] Good.

Are we going to take down his statue? Cause he was a major slave owner. Are we going to take down his statue? So, you know what? It's fine. You are changing history, you are changing culture. You had people, and I'm not talking about the neo-Nazis and the white nationalists, because they should be condemned totally. You had many other people in that group other than neo-Nazis and white nationalists, okay? And the press has treated them absolutely unfairly.

Now, in the other group, also, you had some fine people, but you also had troublemakers, and you see them come with the black outfits and with the helmets and the baseball bats. You had a lot of bad people in the other group, too.[20]

For Cary, still a Bernie Sanders supporter at the time, it was clear that Trump wanted a civil debate on the issue of Confederate statues in public places and was simply concerned about how far the effort would go. Would it eventually require the removal of statues of George Washington and Thomas Jefferson, both slave owners?

By late August 2017, CNN was referring to the "very fine people" statement to support its claim that Trump had *meant* to include neo-Nazis and Ku Klux Klan members—even though in the transcript he said the exact opposite.

Cary called up his friend, Steve, in Georgia, who describes himself as a left-leaning libertarian, and gave him his take on the situation. He was blown away by what Cary told him and said, "That's messed up, man."

With that conversation, Cary had taken his first step away from the CNN madness.

\*\*\*

After the Charlottesville episode, my work at CNN was quiet, but Cary was plagued by a troubling thought: If CNN had lied about Trump's comments about Charlottesville, what else had it lied about?

Cary felt as if he was on a scavenger hunt but didn't really know what he hoped to find. He listened at his desk (with headphones and several open tabs so he could quickly switch if somebody approached) to Trump after coming down the golden escalator at Trump Tower, where he announced that he was running for president, as well as several of his rally speeches. He didn't seem that crazy. Cary understood his argument about the border, as well as his comments that NATO members weren't paying their fair share, and that the United States should avoid "stupid wars." Cary was becoming an "America First" acolyte, which often wreaked havoc with his brain.

"Man, is this real or am I just being sucked in by really good propaganda?" he often asked himself.

Cary went down the rabbit hole of other commentators who were out of favor at CNN, like YouTuber and self-described "disaffected liberal" Tim Pool, author of *Don't Burn This Country* Dave Rubin, political commentator and stand-up comic Steven Crowder, and economist and historian Thomas Sowell.

Cary was still working on his college degree in psychology, and some of the concepts began to bleed over into his political awakening. He thought about the idea of Stockholm syndrome, the propensity of hostage victims to eventually sympathize with their captors. He also read with growing horror the devious way in which domestic abusers twist the minds of their victims to get them to voluntarily disassociate from those people most likely to point out the abuse to the victim.

Was CNN in effect acting as a domestic abuser to half the population, causing them to stop speaking to the other half of the population?

That's how countries disintegrate.

And Cary was beginning to believe that was exactly what CNN was doing.

\*\*\*

Cary continued his work at CNN, covering some fun events, like Groundhog Day in Punxsutawney, Pennsylvania, made famous by the Bill Murray movie of the same name. He doesn't think he's ever been so cold in his entire life.

And yet, he couldn't escape the feeling that he was working for some very dishonest people.

On October 27, 2018, Robert Bowers, a forty-six-year-old man, walked into the Tree of Life synagogue in Pittsburgh, Pennsylvania, and started shooting, killing eleven worshippers and wounding six other people, four of whom were police officers in the process of engaging in a gun battle with Bowers, who eventually surrendered.

Cary got the call shortly after the shooting, and within an hour he was on the road with the satellite truck and a CNN engineer. As later recounted on CNN:

> "They're committing genocide to my people," Bowers told police during the shootout, according to an FBI affidavit. "I just want to kill Jews…"
>
> For weeks before the shooting, Bowers targeted Jews in frequent posts on Gab, a social media platform that bills itself as "the free speech social network." He used anti-Semitic slurs, complained that President Donald Trump was surrounded by too many Jewish people and blamed Jews for helping migrant caravans in Central America.
>
> He also posted pictures of his handgun collection. Bowers had 21 guns registered to his name, said Rep. Mike Doyle, whose district includes Squirrel Hill.[21]

Like he'd raced to the scene in Charlottesville, he was doing the same in Pittsburgh, popping the satellite dish up to get a clear signal and parking the truck close enough to run the cable lines to the talent, which would eventually include Anderson Cooper and Wolf Blitzer.

There was no sense of excitement in getting to the scene, as Cary suspected it would be similar to Charlottesville. This is how CNN reported it at the time:

> Robert Jones, the FBI special agent in charge of the Pittsburgh office, called the shooting "the most horrific crime scene" he'd witnessed in 22 years with the bureau. It began as a peaceful morning as dozens of people filed inside the building to celebrate Shabbat services with three congregations, Tree of Life, Dor Hadash and New Light.

Rabbi Hazzan Jeffrey Myers with the Tree of Life said the shooting began shortly after he started services at 9:45 a.m.

"My holy place has been defiled," he said at Sunday's service. He vowed to rebuild his congregation and called on those in the audience to do their part.[22]

And what would CNN do in response to this evil? Would it try to bring the country together, or would it try to tear it apart? The answer quickly became clear, and Cary could only be ashamed at the small part he played in setting up the narrative for CNN. Here is how President Trump talked about the tragedy:

As you know, earlier today, there was a horrific shooting targeting and killing Jewish Americans at the Tree of Life synagogue in Pittsburgh, Pennsylvania. The shooter is in custody.

And federal authorities have been dispatched to support state and local police and conduct a full and thorough federal investigation. This wicked act of mass murder is pure evil, hard to believe, and frankly, something that is unimaginable. Our nation and the world are shocked and stunned by grief.

This was an anti-Semitic act. You wouldn't think that would be possible in this day and age. But we just don't seem to learn from the past. Our minds cannot comprehend this cruel hate and the twisted malice that could cause a person to unleash such terrible violence during a baby-naming ceremony. This was a baby-naming ceremony, at a sacred house of worship on the holy day of Sabbath.

Anti-Semitism and the widespread persecution of Jews represents one of the ugliest and darkest features of human history. The vile, hate-filled poison of anti-Semitism must be condemned and confronted everywhere and anywhere it appears. There must be no tolerance for anti-Semitism in America or for any form of religious or racial hatred or prejudice.[23]

As with Charlottesville, these were appropriate remarks. Yet, this is how CNN whipped up hatred against Trump when he went to pay his respects at the Tree of Life synagogue, in a story delivered by Miguel Marquez to Jake Tapper on October 30, 2018:

> JAKE TAPPER: Miguel, how are the Pittsburghers you're talking to, how do they feel about the President's visit?
>
> [Marquez was standing on a lawn near a nondescript building among some protestors, one of whom held a sign that read, "Your Hate Speech has Consequences."]
>
> MIGUEL MARQUEZ: Look, Jake, I have not seen a dry eye in this neighborhood all day. People walking their dogs, moving around the neighborhood and now this. That sadness, that absolute shock at what— [camera pans to a crowd of about thirty or forty people, showing, most prominently, the back of a man wearing a blue Service Employees International Union jacket]—at what happened, has turned into anger with news of the President's visit.
>
> [The camera then focuses on a couple with the man holding his toddler daughter in a purple dress and gently bouncing her up and down.]

MARQUEZ: There are several hundred people here at this protest getting ready to march just as the President is expected to land in Pittsburgh and move around the city. [Camera focuses again on the sign "Your Hate Speech has Consequences."] There is a second protest in the neighborhood. President Donald Trump, in this neighborhood, is definitely unwelcome.[24]

Cary kept thinking of the idea of CNN as a domestic abuser of the country, keeping Americans apart, even in times of tragedy.

This was the first time he considered leaving CNN. But he also didn't know if that was enough. What was his responsibility as a citizen? This wasn't about politics. It was about something deeper.

To be citizens in a democracy, people need objective information, but they also need to believe that those with differing opinions are worthy of their attention. That presumption of goodwill about our ideological opposites is a fundamental bedrock of our society.

How could Cary begin the conversation to lessen the hatred and get Americans talking to each other again?

As it would turn out, it was CNN that gave him the opportunity to expose it.

\*\*\*

CNN has a presence at the annual Conservative Political Action Conference (CPAC), and in March 2019 Cary was assigned the job of driving the satellite truck out to the event.

He felt enormous excitement that he'd be around these conservative content creators he'd been secretly following and get the chance to observe them up close. Maybe behind the scenes he'd finally observe their secret racist handshakes and dog whistles and go back to being a good little leftist.

He happened to be walking through Radio Row, where the news channels set up their interviews, and saw James O'Keefe, the founder and public face of Project Veritas, being interviewed by the *Epoch Times*. Cary was familiar with O'Keefe, and when Cary opened his conference program and saw that O'Keefe was scheduled to speak shortly on the main stage, he figured he'd go and listen to him.

After being introduced, James started a talk by putting up an image of a woman, whose face was blurred out, with the caption, "FACEBOOK WHISTLEBLOWER."

> JAMES O'KEEFE: This is a young woman, who a year ago came to me with documents. The documents from inside Facebook showed the company issuing what they call a deboost on their live feed distribution videos. The documents also showed a Troll Report, where they identify keywords, that are not racist, are not extreme, but pretty harmless words. Meme words, words like normie, and lulls, and mainstream media.
>
> This insider lost her job for leaking this information to us. And we got a response from Facebook this week that confirmed they deboosted these livestream videos. She saw them do it against Steven Crowder's page, The Daily Caller's page, and Mike Cernovich's page.
>
> And this comes a year after our investigation showing Twitter shadow-banning. Engineers saying they do in fact shadow-ban and have shadow-banned content from timelines without you knowing it. What's shocking about this Facebook story just released two days ago is that people do not know their content is being deboosted.
>
> People need to understand that all the power resides in these social media companies. Andrew Breitbart said the media is everything. Politics is downstream

from culture. And the culture and the media, it's all in the power of the media.

This heroic whistleblower blew the whistle and lost her job. It's pretty heroic what she did. And this just broke two days ago.[25]

Cary was riveted by this talk, feeling that James was speaking directly to him. O'Keefe had two purposes that day: first to speak to conservatives, then to speak to those beyond the conference who might be working in Big Tech or Big Media, who were observing unethical conduct and wanted to know what to do about it. Near the end of the talk, it was mentioned that James would be signing copies of his book, *American Pravda*, in the main hallway later in the day.

Cary figured this would be his chance to make contact.

\*\*\*

Even though Cary was close to maxing out his credit card, he plunked it down to buy a copy of *American Pravda* and made his way to the exhibition hall.

O'Keefe appeared, took some time to get situated, and took his seat, and the line started to move. Cary was about ten or fifteen people from the front, and there were two to three times the number of people behind him. At best, he'd have twenty or thirty seconds to make his connection with O'Keefe.

Then Cary was directly in front of him. "Who am I making it out to?" he asked, as he took the book from Cary's hands.

"Cary," I said, then added quietly, "I work for a three-letter news agency, and I definitely want to have a conversation."

He looked up, cautiously interested, but still a poker face. "Oh," he replied, "Where do you work?"

"CNN."

He put a hand to his mouth, then softly said, "Oh boy." He quickly pulled out a business card from his front pocket, scribbled his phone number on it, put it in the book, and handed it back to Cary.

Anybody watching the scene might not have even noticed the business card. The words to each other had been few, and the brief interaction didn't seem much different from any of the other people waiting in line.

Cary is not sure what happened when he turned and started walking away, but James must have done something. By the time Cary was walking out the door of the exhibition hall, Spencer Meads, another Project Veritas employee, had found him.

"You want to talk to James?"

"Yeah."

"You work at CNN?"

"I do."

"I need your name."

"I go by Cary Poarch, but my legal name is David Carrington Poarch. I don't know how they might have me listed at CNN."

"Okay," said Spencer, then gave me his phone number.

They talked for a few more minutes; Spencer probably wanted to see if Cary might bolt because he'd been playing some practical joke. Then Spencer said, "All right, Cary. We'll be in touch."

And with that, Spencer walked away.

Cary met Spencer in his hotel room after the conference ended and talked for nearly an hour. The Project Veritas members were interested in what Cary had to say but were cautious. "I never ask a person to go undercover at the first conversation," said James. "This is a big decision. You need to think about it."

They parted that night without Cary making a commitment.

A few weeks later Cary called and said, "I'm ready to do it. I'm ready to wear a camera and record."

\*\*\*

Starting at noon on October 14, 2019, and continuing that week, Project Veritas released a series of tapes based on Cary's undercover filming. The first shock was how CNN president Jeff Zucker was blaming Fox News for the division in the country.

> JEFF ZUCKER: I think what's going on in America now is really, fundamentally, the result of years of fake news conspiracy nonsense from Fox News that has taken root in this country. And I'm dead serious about this. The fake news conspiracy nonsense that Fox has spread for years is now deeply embedded in American society. And at the highest levels of the Republican elected officials, as we've seen with [Senator] Ron Johnson. And frankly, that is beyond destructive for America. And I do not think we should be scared to say so.[26]

Some might say this is a classic case of projection, the kind of thing that a domestic abuser says. The abuser isn't the problem; it's everybody else. And it's vitally important to name enemies, even if they might have previously been friends.

> JEFF ZUCKER: So, I just wanna say this on the [Senator] Lindsey Graham front. I know that there's a lot of people at CNN that are friendly with Lindsey Graham. Time to knock that off and it's time to call him out. And, you know, I think he's under full-time contract now with Fox News. He's done his last 26 interviews in cable news with Fox. Okay? And, so, it's time to seriously call out what's going on here.[27]

Got it? CNN isn't the problem. It's people like Senators Ron Johnson and Lindsey Graham, and that dastardly Fox News. Time to circle the wagons.

But even the CNN employees saw the obvious erosion of standards as Cary had filmed them revealing, such as Patrick Davis, a twenty-five-year employee and manager of field operations for the Washington bureau.

> PATRICK DAVIS: We could be so much better than what we are. And the buck stops with him [Zucker]. And we've had other presidents. Like, I've been through so many presidents now. Some that are so hands off that you don't even hear from them for a month. You know what I mean? He's involved every day, has a plan, whatever. I just don't agree with it.[28]

It was almost pathetic to hear the laments of Patrick Davis. He was a genuinely good person, who had joined a company he believed in; he'd worked his way up, then the company changed. But in one of those twists of fate, it would turn out to be the best thing that ever happened to him.

Others, like Mike Brevna, floor manager at the Washington bureau, saw things in even starker terms:

> MIKE BREVNA: It's the Trump network, dog. It's like everything is all Trump. They not even thinking about anybody else. They sold themselves to the devil. It's sad, because there's so much news going on out there, but they don't cover none of it. All they do is because of sponsors and everything.[29]

Another employee whom Cary caught on camera speaking about the decline of CNN was Scott Garber, a senior field engineer.

SCOTT GARBER: We used to cover news. We used to go out and do the stories. We used to cover shit. You know, we would've sent a crew on that Honduras plane that crashed last weekend. We would've sent a crew down there 'cause there were four Americans, you know. But [hating] Trump is more important.[30]

It's clear that something has gone wrong when the employees of a news organization lament that it no longer covers news.

\*\*\*

Cary became a whistleblower because he saw something wrong and couldn't let it slide and just go on collecting his paycheck. He felt the need to inform his fellow citizens of what he saw. That decision came at a considerable personal cost.

Cary is no longer married to the mother of his child, a loss he continues to feel deeply as she is a wonderful person. They are trying to make it work as coparents of their daughter, and oddly, they seem to be better as friends than they were as husband and wife. However, Cary knows in his bones that if he had not turned whistleblower, they would have been able to make their marriage a successful one.

Many may ask whether he is sorry that he followed the motto of Project Veritas to "Be brave. Do something."

Cary does not regret anything. He is an optimist.

Since his undercover video aired on October 14, 2019, a number of extraordinary events have taken place.

First, in August 2021, Governor Andrew Cuomo of New York resigned from his office due to long-standing sexual harassment allegations. Many claimed he should have been impeached for the death of thousands of elderly New Yorkers in their nursing homes during the COVID-19 crisis. This criticism is understandable, but Governor Cuomo *has* been removed from the political stage—an enormously positive step.

Second, a little over three months later, CNN fired anchor Chris Cuomo, partially for unethical behavior involved in defending his brother, Andrew Cuomo, and for credible allegations of sexual harassment. Chris Cuomo had been the number one anchor on CNN.

Third, in February 2022, CNN president Jeff Zucker resigned for having lied about his affair with a subordinate, Allison Gollust.

Fourth, Allison Gollust resigned that same month, as a CNN internal investigation also found her guilty of unethical behavior related to her communications with Governor Andrew Cuomo.

Fifth, CNN's ratings have shrunk dramatically since the 2020 election, often numbering less than five hundred thousand viewers a night—interestingly enough, a much smaller audience than for the typical *The Joe Rogan Experience* podcast.

With this book, Cary has continued his investigation of his former employer.

There are many more secrets about CNN—you will find many of them in the following pages.

# CHAPTER TWO

# Sex Problems and CNN

Cary will be the first person to admit that the question of sexual behavior and job performance is usually a question best not included in political debates.

The Right can point to the sexual excesses of Presidents John Kennedy and Bill Clinton, while the Left can point to Donald Trump in what he thought was a private conversation with Billy Bush saying that because of his celebrity, he can often grab a woman "by the pussy." It's not clear whether these debates change anybody's mind, and unfortunately there is a tendency among alpha males to act in these ways. And of course, there are men in high public life who carry themselves without a whiff of scandal in the private lives. Whatever one may think of their politics, both Barack Obama and George W. Bush have avoided sex scandals.

However, this book would not be complete without several high-profile public cases, documented in the media, about the sexual behavior of several CNN figures. While the actions of these individuals themselves cannot be attributed in any way to CNN, it's illuminating to see how CNN reacts, sometimes poorly, and other times with actions that—while they may have been slow in coming—are laudable.

\*\*\*

One of the people whom Cary got to know at CNN's Washington, DC, bureau was senior legal analyst Jeffrey Toobin.

On paper, Toobin is a genuinely impressive figure. His mother was a correspondent for ABC and CBS News, while his father was a news producer. He attended Harvard University, covering sports for the *Harvard Crimson*, then graduated magna cum laude from Harvard Law, and was an editor at the *Harvard Law Review*. One of his early jobs was working for Independent Counsel Lawrence Walsh, investigating the Iran-Contra affair during the Reagan presidency, publishing a book about the case against Lieutenant Colonel Oliver North. Toobin worked for three years as an assistant US attorney in Brooklyn, then in 1993 started writing for *The New Yorker*. Toobin gained exceptional notoriety in 1994 with a *New Yorker* article that O. J. Simpson's defense team planned to use to accuse lead detective Mark Fuhrman of planting evidence.[31] In 2002, Toobin started working for CNN. He has written seven books, all of which have been *New York Times* bestsellers.

While Cary was at CNN, Toobin was always on the news, talking about the Russian collusion story and his belief that the Mueller Report would be the end of the Trump presidency. Cary had probably two dozen interactions with Toobin during his time at CNN, and while Toobin seemed to go to great lengths to appear nice, Cary often got the impression that Toobin was like the awkward kid in the schoolyard who didn't know how to act around others. Being from the South, Cary has a pretty good radar to determine when people are being genuinely nice or simply acting that way because it's what society expects. Toobin didn't strike Cary as a warm, open man, and Cary remembers thinking, *There's just something about him I can't put my finger on.*

On several occasions Cary asked people, "Jeff seems like a nice guy, but is there something off about him?"

People would respond with something like, "That's just Jeff. He's been here a long time," and shrug their shoulders.

On October 20, 2020, Jeff Toobin was on a Zoom conference call with colleagues from *The New Yorker*, and they were conducting an election simulation for the upcoming presidential election. As described in *Vice*:

> Both people who spoke on the condition of anonymity in order to speak freely, noted that it was unclear how much each person saw, but both said they saw Toobin jerking off. The two sources described a juncture in the election simulation when there was a strategy session, and the Democrats and Republicans went into their respective break out rooms for about 10 minutes. At that point, they said, it seemed like Toobin was on a second video call. The sources said that when the groups returned from their break out rooms, Toobin lowered the camera. The people said they could see Toobin touching his penis. Toobin then left the call. Moments later, he called back in, seemingly unaware of what his colleagues had been able to see, and the simulation continued.[32]

*The New Yorker* eventually fired Toobin, and CNN put him on indefinite leave. The story generated a lot of coverage, most of it mocking or slightly humorous, with comments such as, "Jeff, couldn't you have just left the room?" However, as Cary read about it, a number of questions sprang to his mind, disrupting the narrative that this had somehow been an accident. First of all, Toobin had pointed the camera to that specific part of his anatomy. And according to the two witnesses, he seemed to be taking another call. Who was on this other call, and why don't we know the answer to that question?

The *New York Post* ran an article a few days later with other details that simply added to the air of creepiness about the man:

Toobin, a 60-year-old longtime married dad with two adult kids by his wife, had a baby with Casey Greenfield, the daughter of one of Toobin's then-CNN colleagues, Jeff Greenfield, in 2009, the New York Times reported.

Casey, who is 14 years younger than Toobin, met the Harvard Law School grad in the Conde Nast cafeteria while she was working as a fact-checker for Glamour magazine, the outlet reported.

Toobin, who has been married to law school sweetheart Amy McIntosh since 1986, at first denied paternity of the baby, before tests showed he was the dad, the Times said.[33]

What a charming man. He has an affair with the daughter of one of his colleagues and, when she gets pregnant, denies he's the father. How's that for honest and ethical? One gets the impression that despite the amount of media attention on Toobin, he's probably still got a lot of skeletons in the closet. But by June 2021, Toobin was back on the air at CNN. As the New York Post reported:

Jeffrey Toobin partied with his colleagues from CNN after the network welcomed him back with open arms following the Zoom masturbation scandal that got him canned from the New Yorker, reports said Wednesday.

"Toobin isn't just back on CNN's airwaves again— he was out mixing and mingling with his colleagues Tuesday night," Politico Playbook wrote Wednesday after CNN brought Toobin back as their chief legal analyst Thursday following an eight-month absence.

Toobin was in Manhattan with a host of CNN big-wigs for a book party celebrating anchor Brian Stelter's newly released tome on former President Donald Trump.[34]

It seems as if people at CNN are not members of the media defending the public, but a group of insiders who protect each other as much as they possibly can.

And in what may have been an unintentionally embarrassing moment, Toobin was on with Anderson Cooper in late November 2021, just as Cooper was breaking news about another scandal, which mixed elements of family loyalty, sexual misbehavior, and journalistic ethics. The story concerned the collusion between anchor Chris Cuomo and his brother, New York Governor Andrew Cuomo while Andrew was unsuccessfully fighting off allegations of sexual harassment. Because he was a member of the media, Chris Cuomo should not have been privately assisting his brother in private while also reporting on the Governor. As a result of his actions, Chris Cuomo, was fired for violating the canons of journalism. As Fox News reported:

> CNN's Jeffrey Toobin, who recently took several months off amid a scandal of his own, had a front-row seat on Tuesday when Anderson Cooper awkwardly addressed the suspension of his primetime colleague Chris Cuomo, who was benched amid revelations of his deep involvement in his brother's scandals earlier this year.

> "Some news about this network," Cooper told CNN viewers after wrapping up a discussion with the network's top legal analyst, sidelined from last October until June over his Zoom masturbation incident, who was still visible on screen.

"It involves Chris Cuomo, the host of 'Cuomo Prime Time.' New documents released this week indicated that Chris was more intimately involved than previously known in helping his brother, former New York Governor Andrew Cuomo craft a defense amid a flurry of sexual misconduct allegations," Cooper said as the camera cut away from Toobin to focus solely on the "AC 360" host.[35]

Sometimes the bad luck just seems to come in waves. And as much as this may have been an unfortunate trifecta of Jeffrey Toobin, Andrew Cuomo, and Chris Cuomo, it points out a disturbing pattern of hypocrisy at the worst and, at best, a failure of the newsgathering process.

***

How did Governor Andrew Cuomo get away with his bad behavior for so many years in public life, and how did CNN (as well as other media outlets) so badly miss the story? Or was it that they had intentionally avoided it?

If you want the most complete and unbiased account of Governor Andrew Cuomo's behavior, as well as how much his brother, CNN anchor Chris Cuomo, assisted his efforts to avoid detection, you'd probably want to turn to the one-hundred-and-sixty-five-page report that New York Attorney General Leticia James released on August 3, 2021. The executive summary gave a brief overview of the findings:

> Specifically, we [the report's authors] find that the Governor sexually harassed a number of current and former New York State employees by, among other things, engaging in unwelcome and nonconsensual touching, as well as making numerous offensive comments of a suggestive and sexual nature that created a hostile work environment for women. Our

investigation revealed that the Governor's sexually harassing behavior was not limited to members of his own staff, but extended to other State employees, including a State Trooper on his protective detail and members of the public. We also conclude that the Executive Chamber's culture—one filled with fear and intimidation, while at the same time normalizing the Governor's frequent flirtations and gender-based comments—contributed to the conditions that allowed the sexual harassment to occur and persist.[36]

According to the executive summary, Governor Cuomo harassed members of his staff, a trooper in his protective detail, and members of the public. Would any large-state Republican governor have been able to avoid detection by CNN for so long, especially if that governor's brother worked for the network? To be fair, Governor Cuomo and his staff probably engaged in numerous efforts to keep such behavior quiet, but with CNN being a news organization with a significant presence in New York, its failure to detect (or report) even a hint of such behavior is extremely troubling.

Aside from the allegations of sexual harassment, probably the most concerning allegation is contained in the second footnote to the report, which reads:

Many of the individuals we interviewed during our investigation expressed concern and fear over retaliation and requested that, to the extent possible, their identities not be disclosed. Thus, we have sought to anonymize individuals as much as possible, while ensuring the Report's findings and the bases for our conclusions can be fully understood. We have not anonymized individuals whose identities are already publicly known, individuals whose conduct is implicated in the sexual harassment and retaliation allegations, or those who did not raise any concerns about retaliation.[37]

Perhaps part of the explanation for Governor Cuomo's ability to keep these allegations silent for so many years is the culture of fear and intimidation that he fostered; yet, the failure of CNN to discover this cabal located at the very top of the New York state government is genuinely puzzling.

In total, eleven women came forward to complain of Governor Cuomo's harassment. The woman identified as Executive Assistant #1 described a series of escalating sexual comments, innuendo, and inappropriate touching, culminating in what can only be imagined as a truly embarrassing and stereotypical display of predatory behavior by a male boss at the governor's New York State Executive Mansion. According to the report:

> On November 16, 2020, Stephanie Benton, the Director of the Governor's Offices, asked Executive Assistant #1 to assist the Governor at the Executive Mansion. The Blackberry PIN [personal identification number] messages that the PSU uses to announce visitors to the Executive Mansion confirm that Executive Assistant #1 was called to the Executive Mansion and arrived there on November 16. As Executive Assistant #1 finished her assignment and prepared to leave the Governor's personal office, on the second floor of the Mansion, and return to the Capitol, the Governor pulled Executive Assistant #1 in for a close hug.

> Executive Assistant #1 was conscious that the door to the Governor's office (facing out into the hallway on the second floor) was open at the time. Executive Assistant #1 stepped away from the Governor and said, "You're going to get us in trouble." To which the

Governor replied, "I don't care," and slammed the door shut. Executive Assistant #1 testified that the Governor's demeanor at the time "wasn't like 'ha ha,' it was like, 'I don't care.' … It was like in this—at that moment he was sexually driven. I could tell the way he said it, I could tell."

The governor then returned to Executive Assistant #1 and slid his hand up her blouse, and grabbed her breast, "cup[ping her] breast" over her bra. Executive Assistant #1 testified:

I mean it was—he was like cupping my breast. He cupped my breast. I have to tell you it was—at the moment I was in such shock that I could just tell you that I just remember looking down, seeing his hand, seeing the top of my bra and I remember it was like a little even the cup—the kind of bra that I had to the point I could tell you doesn't really fit me properly, it was just a little loose, I just remember seeing exactly that.

In response, Executive Assistant #1 pulled away from the governor and said, "You're crazy." She testified:

At that moment it was so quick and he didn't say anything and I just remember thinking to myself, oh my God, and I remember stopping and him not saying anything and I remember I walked out and he didn't say anything and I didn't say anything.

I remember walking down the back stairs, escorting myself out the front door, going back to my car, taking a deep breath and saying to myself, okay, everything that just happened I have now to pretend like it didn't just happen. Go back to the Capitol and sit at my desk and continue with my afternoon.[38]

The picture painted of Governor Cuomo as a pathetic, lonely man going after a young executive assistant is genuinely disturbing. As a Democrat, he'd pledged to respect women, and yet the situation he'd engineered, having her come to the Executive Mansion, and his position of authority over her lay waste to any claim that this is an encounter between two consenting adults. While most Americans don't believe in snooping too much into a person's private life, when it concerns an abuse of power in order to pursue a sexual relationship with a subordinate, most members of the public will rightfully condemn such behavior.

One of the truly bizarre examples of Governor Cuomo's behavior was his sexual harassment of a state trooper on his Personal Service Unit (PSU). As described in the report:

> Trooper #1 described the Governor's behavior toward her after she joined the PSU as generally "flirtatious" and "creepy."

> Trooper #1 described a series of interactions—both comments and physical touching—that she found inappropriate and offensive. Trooper #1's testimony made clear that although the Governor's conduct made her uncomfortable, she did not feel she could safely report or rebuff the conduct because, based on her experience and discussions with others in the PSU, she feared retaliation and believed her career success hinged on whether the Governor liked her. She explained, "[w]ithin the PSU, it's kind of known that the Governor gives the seal of approval who gets promoted and who doesn't within the PSU." She further explained that members of the PSU gave her

pointers on how to keep the Governor happy, which included "always have an answer, don't tell him no and whatever he wants, make it happen."[39]

It can be daunting to catalogue all the things wrong with this description. One might be tempted to think that the worst of it was the governor's "flirtatious" and "creepy" behavior. But what is equally disturbing is the corruption of the Personal Service Unit into a "Make the Governor Happy Unit," rather than a professional protection detail.

Further details paint a picture of an almost Mafia-like code of silence in the New York state government, rather than an open, democratic, and benevolent group of public servants:

> Later, on August 13, 2019, the Governor asked Trooper #1 questions about her attire while she was driving him to an event. Specifically, the Governor asked her, "why don't you wear a dress?" Trooper #1 replied that it was because she wears a gun and would not have anywhere to put the gun if she wore a dress. According to Trooper #1, the Governor than asked why she wore dark colors. At that point, the Detail Commander, who was also in the Governor's car, interjected and noted that PSU members wear business attire.

> After she left the car, Trooper #1 testified she received a PIN from the Detail Commander that said, "stays in the truck." Which Trooper #1 understood to mean that she should not repeat conversations that occurred in the Governor's car. Trooper #1 noted that before she received this PIN, she had already told the Trooper in the tail car (the car that follows the car with the Governor) about the conversations in

the Governor's car, including saying, "[O]h my God, can you believe the Governor asked me why I don't wear a dress?" She testified that after she received the PIN message, she realized she "messed up" by telling the Trooper in the tail car about the conversations in the Governor's car, and stated that the PIN message "silenced" her.[40]

As a person from a working-class background, Cary can't help but be profoundly saddened by the situation described. When you are just hanging on financially, you often believe deeply that if you just work hard enough you will find yourself with a good job and honorable employers. Cary thinks of those state troopers, people like those with whom he grew up, working hard, getting to a prestigious detail working for the governor of New York, only to find that they need to cover up for the governor's bad behavior. In the Mafia, the code of silence is called *omertà*.

Those troopers entered law enforcement to go after bad guys and protect the good guys. Instead, they found themselves protecting a bad guy, who unfortunately was the leader of their state. As with Executive Assistant #1, the governor's unwelcome comments escalated to unwelcome touching:

The first time Trooper #1 recalls being touched in an unwelcome way by the Governor is when Trooper #1 was at the Governor's New York City Office and was escorting him upstairs in the elevator with Senior Investigator #1. She stated that, as is typical when riding the elevator with the Governor, she stood in front of the door, and the Governor stood behind her. As Trooper #1, Senior Investigator #1, and the Governor were riding the elevator up, the Governor placed his finger on the top of her neck and ran his finger down the center of her spine midway down her back, and said to Trooper #1, "Hey, you."

Trooper #1 also testified about a time when the Governor kissed her during the summer of 2019. Trooper #1 was stationed outside the Mt. Kisco residence and approached the Governor in the driveway to ask if he needed anything. At this point the Governor responded, "Can I kiss you?" Trooper #1 testified, "I remember just freezing, being—in the back of my head, I'm like, oh, how do I say no politely because in my head if I said no, he's going to take it out on the detail. And now I'm on the bad list." Unsure what to do, she replied, "Sure." The Governor then proceeded to kiss Trooper #1 on the cheek and said something to the effect of "oh, I'm not supposed to do that" or "unless that's against the rules."

Another member of the PSU observed the interaction and corroborated the kiss in an interview with us. After the incident, he joked to Trooper #1 that the Governor had never asked to kiss him.[41]

When people ask Cary why he was the first person to stand up at CNN (technically working as a contractor) and wear a wire to document what he saw and heard inside the organization, he points to examples like this incident. If a passing motorist had stopped the governor's car, got out, and asked to kiss the Trooper, she would've likely arrested the man or read him the riot act. But since Cuomo was her boss, the only thing Trooper #1 could think to do was say "sure," while her male partner was impotently reduced to joking that "the Governor had never asked to kiss him."

Are people still too intimidated to report bad behavior by their bosses?

Apparently, they are.

***

While it may not be surprising that a powerful public figure like Governor Cuomo attempts to sexually harass his staff and those around him, it boggles the mind to read the account of Virginia Limmiatis, a woman who simply met Governor Cuomo at a public event. From the report of the attorney general:

> In May 2017, Virginia Limmiatis attended a conservation event in upstate New York on behalf of her employer ("Energy Company"), at which the Governor spoke. After the event Ms. Limmiatis stood in a rope line to meet with the Governor, along with other attendees. She wore a shirt that had the name of Energy Company written across the chest....
>
> When the Governor reached her, Ms. Limmiatis held out her hand for a handshake. The Governor walked up close to Ms. Limmiatis and pressed his first two fingers of his right hand on each letter of the Energy Company's name printed across the chest of Ms. Limmiatis' shirt. The Governor pressed his fingers on each letter before sliding his fingers to the next letter, while saying "[Energy Company] I know you." The Governor leaned in so his cheek was touching Ms. Limmiatis' cheek and said something along the lines of, "I'm going to say I see a spider on your shoulder." Ms. Limmiatis looked down to see that there was no spider or bug on her, but the Governor brushed his hand in the area between her shoulder and breast below her collarbone. Ms. Limmiatis testified that she was too shocked and appalled during the interaction to say anything, and understood the Governor knew

he had "done something wrong and that he had to create a cover story."[42]

Creepy Governor Cuomo does what he wants to a woman in a rope line for a cheap thrill, and nobody seems to care. Even when Limmiatis told her boss, he "did not raise the option of reporting what happened to the Energy Company or the Executive Chamber...."[43] Once again, when a regular citizen, this time in the form of a supervisor for the "Energy Company," gets the chance to take on the corrupt and powerful, he takes a pass.

And after doing an exhaustive review of the "Executive Chamber" put in place by Governor Cuomo, this is what the report's authors wrote:

> We find that all of these aspects of the Executive Chamber's culture—*e.g.*, the use of fear, intimidation and retribution, the acceptance of everyday flirtation and gender-based comments by the Governor as just "old-fashioned," the overriding focus on loyalty and protecting the Governor and attacking any detractors, and the reliance on loyal confidantes regardless of their official role in State government (or lack thereof)—contributed to creating an environment where the Governor's sexually harassing conduct was allowed to flourish and persist. It also interfered with the Executive Chamber's ability—and responsibility— to respond to allegations of sexual harassment in a proper way by taking them seriously, reporting them, and having GOER [Governor's Office of Employee Relations] investigate them. Instead, whether driven by fear or blinded by loyalty, the senior staff of the Executive Chamber (and the Governor's select group of outside confidantes) looked to protect the Governor and found ways not to believe or credit

those who stepped forward to make or support allegations against him.[44]

And who was part of this "select group of outside confidantes?"

No less than Andrew's brother, the CNN anchor himself, Chris Cuomo.

Let's take a look at Chris Cuomo's actions as his brother sought to fend of these sexual harassment claims.

\*\*\*

How deeply involved was CNN anchor Chris Cuomo and presenter of *Cuomo Prime Time* in helping his brother, Governor Andrew Cuomo, evade responsibility for sexual harassment? Well, we don't have to guess, as the New York Attorney General's Office went a long way toward answering that question by releasing a series of text messages between Chris Cuomo and Melissa DeRosa, the former secretary to Governor Cuomo.

The portion released covered a period between February 27, 2021, and March 15, 2021.

The exchange released begins with DeRosa forwarding a tweet by Jesse McKinley, Albany bureau chief for the *New York Times*, which read:

> EXCLUSIVE/BREAKING: A 25-year-old former aide to @NYGovCuomo told the @nytimes the Governor sexually harassed, asking if she had sex with older men, among other claims. [Later revealed to be Charlotte Bennett.]

> [Andrew] Cuomo says was a mentor, "never made advances," or acted inappropriately.

> CHRIS CUOMO: What happened to the statement?

DEROSA: I'm on with the AG [attorney general].

CUOMO: Here's what he [Governor Cuomo] should have said:

*I have carefully considered Ms. [Charlotte] Bennet's [sic] statement and my own conduct, I don't dispute that our conversation was as she reports. I also do not dispute that my words and supervisory position may have created a hostile work environment. I apologize to Ms. Bennett and will promptly seek to personally communicate my apology to her. I also apologize to the people of New York State, who have a right to better conduct from their Governor. This will not happen again.*[45]
(Italics added.)

From the outset of these text messages between Melissa DeRosa and Chris Cuomo, it's clear that Chris Cuomo is essentially acting as a communications director and strategist for his brother, rather than staying out of the dispute, as would be expected of a journalist with a high-profile sibling. Chris Cuomo's critique and stage directions continue.

CHRIS CUOMO: Andrew Cuomo's poor statement, annotated:

Questions have been raised about some of my past interactions with people in the office. *[Questions have not been raised; accusations have been made.]* I never intended to offend anyone or cause any harm. *[No one says he intended to offend or harm. What he's accused of is creating a hostile work environment, which is judged objectively by the natural meaning of his words and conduct, not what he now says he intended.]* I spend most of my life at work and colleagues are often also personal friends. *[It's perhaps true that work colleagues are personal friends, but most supervisors know that many issues may arise from personal friendships with work subordinates.]* (Italics added.)

At work sometimes I think I am being playful and make jokes that I think are funny, I do, on occasion, tease people in what I think is a good natured way. I do it in public and in private. You have seen me do it at briefings hundreds of times. I have teased people about their personal....[46]

One can't really say that Chris Cuomo's analysis of the situation is wrong. Despite the fact that conservatives often denigrate Chris as the "Fredo" of the Cuomo family, after the fictional Fredo from the *Godfather* movies, the simpleminded son of Marlon Brando's powerful Mafia don, Cuomo seems to be a sharp-eyed critic of the trouble bearing down on his brother, as well as pointing out the mistakes he was making.

The series of texts released by the attorney general can be confusing, which is why the authors must add explanations—so the reader can understand them. The next series of text messages are between March 2, 2021, and March 5, 2021, beginning with this text from Cuomo.

CHRIS CUOMO: Godddam. I panic every fucking time I see your name. The talk is precarious. I worry about this "if investigations prove allegations he has to go."

CUOMO: Please let me help with the prep.

MELISSA DEROSA: Just came in. [DeRosa is referring to an email from CBS News with a request for a comment from Governor Cuomo.]

"Hi Richard and Elkan [Cuomo staff members],

We are planning on imminently airing Norah's on-camera interview with Gov. Cuomo's former executive assistant Charlotte Bennet [sic]. As such, we would like to give Gov. Cuomo the opportunity to respond to allegations made by Ms. Bennett.

Specifically, we would like Gov. Cuomo to address the following: Gov. Cuomo's views on his relationship with Ms. Bennett."

CUOMO: Thoughts?

CUOMO: Called. I have a lead on the wedding girl.

CUOMO: www.newsweek.com/women-accusing-cuomo-wont-come-out-top-opinion-1573595[47]

What these texts clearly establish is that Chris Cuomo actively sought out to aid his brother, despite that being a clear violation of journalistic ethics. In fact, the opinion piece he texted to DeRosa (Andrew Cuomo's secretary) was interesting in its approach, as the title "Women Accusing Cuomo Won't Come Out on Top," by Froma Harrop, suggested an avenue of attack differing sharply from typical Democratic talking points:

Three women have accused New York's Andrew Cuomo of sexual harassment. These complaints center largely around unsolicited shows of affection.

He [Governor Cuomo] very well may have said the inappropriate things being reported, but none of the women were physically harmed by what at most was unwanted flirtation. You have to ask: What will these displays of fragility do to the women's careers? Little that's good, unless they plan to seek tenure in a department of gender studies.

"I understood the governor wanted to sleep with me," said Charlotte Bennett, a former aide, "and felt horribly uncomfortable and scared." A grown woman getting "scared" by a come-on? From a New Yorker, no less?

Wanting the world to know of her torment, Bennett made herself available to the media, done in cat-eye makeup. Basically, that involves a vixenish wing of eyeliner swooshing to the outer corner.[48]

Is this the best that Chris Cuomo can come up with? A twenty-five-year-old woman should expect to be hit on by her powerful sixty-two-year-old boss, and if she does complain, she'd better be wearing a demure type of eyeliner? It seems this may indicate the Empire State Democrats' true colors on women's rights.

Several texts went back and forth between DeRosa and Cuomo about various opinion pieces, when on March 7, 2021, it seemed as if the situation had taken a turn for the worse.

> MELISSA DEROSA: Rumor going around from Politico 1-2 more ppl coming out tomorrow.
> [Referring to another news story.]
>
> DEROSA: Can you check your sources?
>
> CHRIS CUOMO: On it.
>
> CUOMO: No one has heard that yet.
>
> DEROSA: K.

DEROSA: www.dailymail.co.uk/tvshowbiz/article-9336481/Alec-Baldwin-shares-14-minute-rant-hitting-cancel-culture-arguing-process.html

CUOMO: My friend asked him to do it. Very close to him.[49]

Chris Cuomo's violation of journalistic ethics becomes exceedingly clear in this exchange. Cuomo was using his "sources" to ferret out information, and in case the Cuomo brothers needed any celebrity help, actor Alec Baldwin could be instructed to jump to Governor Cuomo's defense. This is a classic case of "muddying the waters" to distract the public from the main issue, which was Governor Cuomo's behavior. Chris Cuomo was clearly steering the news coverage about his brother.

On March 9, 2021, journalist Ronan Farrow, who had exposed Harvey Weinstein's sexual harassment of a multitude of women, seemed ready to release more incriminating material.

MELISSA DEROSA: Rumor about Ronan getting ready to move.

DEROSA: Can you check your sources?

DEROSA: Do u see this?

DEROSA: https://www.timesunion.com/news/article/Cuomo-faces-new-allegation-of-sexual-harassment-16011424.php

CHRIS CUOMO: Why didn't you tell him about potential ATU [Amalgamated Transit Union] interview with 6? [News station.]

DEROSA: I asked u not to say anything until I talked to him.

CUOMO: That was a day ago. Stop hiding shit.

DEROSA: I told him it is a suspicion.

CUOMO: You need to trust me, Lis, and Jeff more. Not these other people. We are making mistakes we can't afford.[50]

When on a sinking ship, there's often little one can do to prolong the inevitable. And, despite these efforts on his behalf, on August 24, 2021, Governor Cuomo resigned from office. On December 4, 2021, anchor Chris Cuomo was fired by CNN. As reported by the *New York Times*:

> The star anchor Chris Cuomo was fired by CNN on Saturday, completing a stunning downfall for the network's top-rated host amid a continuing inquiry into his efforts to help his brother, Andrew M. Cuomo, then the governor of New York, stave off sexual harassment accusations.
>
> The anchor was suspended on Tuesday after testimony and text messages released by the New York attorney general revealed a more intimate and engaged role in his brother's political affairs than the network said it had previously known.
>
> On Wednesday, Debra S. Katz, a prominent employment lawyer, informed CNN of a client with an allegation of sexual misconduct against Chris Cuomo. Ms. Katz said in a statement on Saturday that the allegation against the anchor, which was made by a former

junior colleague at another network, was "unrelated to the Gov. Andrew Cuomo matter."[51]

The presumption of innocence is an important concept in our society, but once an investigation has been conducted and patterns of conduct established, we can start to feel more comfortable expressing opinions about the actions of certain individuals. For Governor Andrew Cuomo, the evidence of sexual harassment and the creation of a cabal of loyal confidantes who would ruthlessly enforce his will was so overwhelming that the governor felt he had no other political option other than resignation.

For CNN anchor Chris Cuomo, the evidence must have appeared so overwhelming to the network, that the newsman had violated journalistic ethics in a way so egregious, that it had no other choice but to fire him. The allegations of sexual misconduct against Chris Cuomo can only be called allegations at this time. But they fit the same well-documented pattern of his brother, the former governor of New York, Andrew Cuomo.

While one may speculate how much CNN knew about any of these situations, the question remains how the network that calls itself "the most trusted name in news" had missed (or ignored) two such enormous stories in its own backyard.

\*\*\*

The parade of bad news about CNN employees and sex problems continued at the network.

On December 10, 2021, a week after CNN fired Chris Cuomo, the FBI arrested the former lead producer for Chris Cuomo, John Griffin, on three counts of using interstate commerce in an attempt to entice minors to engage in unlawful sexual activity. As reported by CNN:

> Connecticut man John Griffin was arrested Friday and charged with three counts of using a facility of interstate commerce to attempt to entice minors to

engage in unlawful sexual activity, the United States Attorney's Office for the District of Vermont said in a news release.

Griffin, 44, had been a producer with CNN for about eight years.

"The charges against Mr. Griffin are deeply disturbing," a spokesperson for the network said in a statement Saturday. "We only learned of his arrest yesterday afternoon and have suspended him pending investigation."

The charges stem from conversations between Griffin and the purported parents of minor daughters, in which he allegedly tried to persuade them to "allow him to train their daughters to be sexually submissive," as well as an incident in which prosecutors allege unlawful sexual activity occurred with a 9-year-old girl, the news release said.[52]

The press release from the United States Attorney's Office further detailed the actions of Cuomo's former producer:

The indictment also includes specific allegations that Griffin attempted to entice two other children over the internet to engage in sexual activity. In April of 2020, Griffin proposed to engage in a "virtual training session" over a video chat that would include him instructing the mother and her 14-year-old daughter to remove their clothing and touch each other at his direction. In June of 2020, Griffin proposed to a purported mother of a 16-year-old daughter that she take a "little mother-daughter trip" to Griffin's Ludlow ski house for sexual training involving the child.[53]

The regular person hears of such behavior and is appalled. It's difficult to imagine which punishment could fit the crime of abusing a child in such a manner. However, each count carries with it a ten-year mandatory minimum sentence and a maximum sentence of life imprisonment, so perhaps there will be some measure of justice in this case.

\*\*\*

After escaping Washington, DC, to Florida after the release of Cary's undercover Project Veritas story about CNN, he should probably tell you a good deal of what happened.

Rebecca and Cary were married in March 2020, just as COVID was closing down the nation, and their daughter Emma was born a few weeks later, healthy and happy.

Cary got another sales job in the telecom industry shortly after they arrived in Florida, and it was a decent job. However, after a year, Cary got a job with a different company for more money. But after spending so much time being undercover at CNN for Project Veritas, he missed the rush and the feeling of doing something genuinely worthwhile with his life.

One of the things that James O'Keefe had put together was something of a traveling road show for the Project Veritas whistleblowers, and it made Cary want to be with the group on a more permanent basis. Sometime around April 2021, Cary directly asked the chief operating officer of Project Veritas whether they might have a job for him. The interview process was long and arduous, taking several months, but in late June, Cary was officially hired by Project Veritas with the job title of investigative journalist. In addition, he'd be part of the team monitoring the tip line for potential whistleblowers, building emotional rapport with these individuals, deciding whether there was a story in what they described, which documents they might have to support their claims, and whether they'd be willing to wear a hidden camera. In many ways one might say that Cary had become the "tip of the spear" for Project Veritas.

In late July 2021 at FreedomFest in Rapid City, South Dakota, he met Kent Heckenlively, who had coauthored two books by former Project Veritas whistleblowers, and asked if he might help with Cary's story. Kent was a charming guy, intelligent, interested in Cary's thoughts, and quick with a laugh: the perfect collaborator. "Big pharma, Google, and Facebook," he said, referencing the subject of his previous books. "Sounds like CNN should be next on the list."

Cary would soon be drawn back into another CNN story.

\*\*\*

As bad as the story was of Chris Cuomo's CNN producer John Griffin, the story of Rick Saleeby, the senior producer for CNN's *The Lead with Jake Tapper*, was even worse. Cary had had some interactions with Saleeby when Cary worked at CNN, and Saleeby always given him the creeps.

A former lover of Saleeby had contacted Project Veritas stating that Saleeby was calling her and telling her his fantasies of performing sex acts on his fiancée's underage daughter. What he said, and what Project Veritas recorded, was truly sickening. In addition, Saleeby was often telling this former lover that, in view of the fact that he'd given her money in the past, she should send him nude pictures of herself with her underage daughter.

On December 15, 2021, Project Veritas released the phone calls between Saleeby and his former lover, and they were genuinely stomach-turning. Project Veritas had acted so quickly, not only to alert the mother in the interest of protecting the young girl, but also to put pressure on law enforcement to act quickly on what appeared to be an imminent threat to the girl.

The fiancée quickly broke up with Saleeby and filed a protective order against him. The Fairfax County Police Department released a statement on the case in late December, which read:

The Fairfax County Police Department has launched an investigation into serious allegations involving potential juvenile victims. Detectives assigned to the Child Exploitation Squad of the Major Crimes Bureau are leading the investigation. While we will eventually be transparent about our findings, safeguarding the personal privacy of victims and witnesses as well as maintaining the integrity of our criminal investigation are of paramount importance.[54]

What was probably the most rewarding aspect of this case was the thank-you letter that Saleeby's former fiancée sent to Project Veritas a few days after the story broke. With her permission, Project Veritas redacted some of her letter, and published it for the benefit of all those who'd been so deeply concerned by the story. The young girl's mother wrote:

I wanted to reach out to sincerely thank you again. I am very grateful toward you guys and everything you've done for me and my children. Our world has just been completely flipped upside down, but none of that matters. We are all safe. I'm hoping, praying, and pushing for charges to be brought against him, so he can never do this to another child/family again.

I want the public and any predators to know, without a shadow of doubt, that I will go to the absolute ends of the earth to protect my babies. And I am tremendously grateful that you guys have saved us all from him.

Despite the hardships ahead, I am going to continue to sit with these feelings of gratitude toward you guys and the woman who provided you with the information. Gratitude will get us through to the other side of all this.

Thank you from the bottom of my heart and Merry Christmas.[55]

It made Cary feel like he was on the side of the good guys.

However, he doesn't know if he can draw any conclusions about whether CNN attracts people with such strange behaviors or if it's simply an unusual series of coincidences. Maybe something similar will one day hit Fox News or the *New York Times*.

But when looking at the weird behavior of Jeffrey Toobin; the actions of Governor Andrew Cuomo; how his brother, Chris Cuomo, a journalist, so quickly abandoned any objectivity to smear the women who accused the governor; and the obsession with underage girls by producers for Chris Cuomo and Jake Tapper, Cary wonders if he's merely scratched the surface of what's really taking place at CNN and possibly at many other major institutions in the country.

# CHAPTER THREE

# The Fall of Jeff Zucker

On February 2, 2022, CNN president Jeff Zucker submitted his resignation effective immediately. As reported by CNN journalists Brian Stelter and Oliver Darcy:

> Zucker's stunning announcement came less than two months after he fired prime time anchor Chris Cuomo for improperly advising his brother, then-New York Gov. Andrew Cuomo, about how to address sexual misconduct allegations.

> "As part of the investigation into Chris Cuomo's tenure at CNN, I was asked about a consensual relationship with my closest colleague, someone I have worked with for more than 20 years," Zucker told employees in a memo. "I acknowledged that the relationship evolved in recent years. I was required to disclose when it began but I didn't. I was wrong. As a result, I am resigning today."

Zucker did not name his colleague, but the relationship is with Allison Gollust, his key lieutenant for the last two decades. Gollust is remaining at CNN.[56]

As the poet Sir Walter Scott wrote in the nineteenth century, "Oh, what a tangled web we weave when first we practice to deceive." The domino of resignations cascaded from Governor Cuomo to CNN anchor Chris Cuomo to CNN president Jeff Zucker.

And when did Zucker's relationship with Gollust begin?

Zucker noted that even though he had worked with Allison Gollust for more than twenty years, the relationship had only "evolved in recent years." But Allison, in a statement of her own, provided a bit more clarity. According to Stelter and Darcy:

> Zucker and Gollust began working together at NBC in 1998. They rose through the ranks at the network together, and when Zucker joined CNN, Gollust was among his first hires. Just before coming to CNN Gollust had worked briefly as communications director for Andrew Cuomo. She is currently executive vice president and chief marketing officer at CNN.
>
> In a statement of her own, Gollust said, "Jeff and I have been close friends and professional partners for over 20 years. Recently, our relationship changed during COVID. I regret we didn't disclose it at the right time. I'm incredibly proud of my time at CNN and look forward to continuing the great work we do every day."[57]

But wait! There is another bombshell. Gollust used to work as communications director for Governor Cuomo, whose indiscretions started this entire avalanche. No writer of fiction could ever claim such an implausible chain of events. But like any good piece of fiction, many were left wondering which other secrets were yet to be disclosed.

According to Gollust, the relationship "changed during COVID," so that is sometime around March 2020, when the nationwide lockdowns began.

Is that the end of the story?

These long-time coworkers began an affair, and their technical failure to report their relationship ended with Zucker's *voluntary* resignation—the selfless act of a good man falling on his sword?

And yet, former NBC *Today Show* reporter Katie Couric painted a much different picture of the relationship between Jeff Zucker and Allison Gollust in the early 2000s, when all three of them worked together at NBC.

> Couric, the former "Today" show star who worked under Zucker when he helmed the NBC morning ratings juggernaut in the early 2000s, once observed in her memoir, "Going There" that he and Gollust were "joined at the hip."
>
> She noted that Zucker and Gollust not only worked together but their families lived a floor away from each other in the same apartment building while they were both married to their spouses....
>
> "She [Gollust] and her husband and kids had moved into the apartment right above Jeff and Caryn's—everyone who heard about their cozy arrangement thought it was super strange," Couric wrote.[58]

Couric's suspicion is that Jeff Zucker and Allison Gollust were having an affair decades before they officially disclosed it in February 2022.

The suddenness of Zucker's fall caught many by surprise, especially as CNN was in the middle of some very delicate negotiations. As detailed by Stelter and Darcy:

WarnerMedia [CNN's parent company] is in the process of merging with Discovery. Many media observers thought Zucker was in line for a promotion once the deal is complete. That is not the only reason this is a pivotal time for the network: CNN plans to launch an ambitious streaming service, CNN+, in the spring, and it also needs to roll out a new 9 p.m. program to replace Cuomo.[59]

Can anybody say "really bad timing?" Not only had CNN lost its superstar anchor, Chris Cuomo, but it had now lost the head of the network.

From the outside it didn't seem like there were any real villains, just an incredibly embarrassing series of revelations. And yet from the reporting by Stelter and Darcy, there did seem to be a villain—and it was Chris Cuomo, CNN's former anchor:

Before taking action, CNN retained Cravath, a white-shoe law firm, to review the Cuomo matter.

When Cuomo was fired, CNN said that Cravath's findings alone "were cause enough to terminate." But the network also said it had received an allegation of sexual misconduct from a "former junior colleague" against Chris Cuomo. Though Cuomo denied the allegation, a CNN spokesperson said at the time, "When new allegations came to us this week, we took them seriously and saw no reason to delay taking immediate action."

Cravath has continued its probe, according to sources familiar with the matter. One complicating factor is Cuomo's ongoing legal battle with CNN, which is apparently why Zucker was questioned about his relationship with Gollust, one of the sources said.[60]

Was Zucker's forced resignation a direct result of Chris Cuomo's vendetta against him for being fired? Within hours of the announcement of Zucker's resignation it seemed the campaign to rehabilitate him had swung into full force, complete with the appropriate narrative. On the show *Newsroom*, CNN anchor Alisyn Camerota said:

> I want to say something personal for a moment. I feel it deeply personally, but I think I speak for all of us and our colleagues. This is an incredible loss. Jeff is a remarkable person and an incredible leader. He has this uncanny ability to make, I think, every one of us feel special and valuable in our own way even though he is managing an international news organization of thousands of people. I just know he had this unique ability to make us feel special. I don't think that comes around all the time. I think, again, it's a terrible loss. I just think it's so regrettable how it happened. If what you are reporting is true, these are two consenting adults who are both executives. That they can't have a private relationship feels wrong on some level.[61]

This attempted emotional manipulation by Alisyn Camerota is genuinely remarkable. She is not acting as an objective news reporter. She's attempting to rehabilitate the reputation of her powerful boss who disobeyed his own rules, in addition to setting half the country against the other with his anti-Trump bias. Yes, it is just as bad as Governor Cuomo being forced to resign for his sexual behavior, rather than the thousands of deaths he caused by sending elderly COVID patients back into nursing homes, rather than quarantining them in facilities that had been provided by the federal government.

But still, it was a victory for those who wanted objective journalism.

Into this morality play comes Brian Stelter, stepping right in after Camerota makes her viewers feel sad, to turn that sadness into anger by pointing the finger at the true author of this tragedy, Chris Cuomo. As reported by Breitbart:

> Media reporter Brian Stelter said, "Chris Cuomo was fired in December, and he's not going out quietly. He was fired, and there were reports he was not going to be paid the millions of dollars on the remainder of his contract. As a source said earlier today, he was trying to burn the place down. He was going to court trying to burn the place down and claiming he had incriminating information on Zucker and Gollust."[62]

There are the facts from "the most trusted name in news." Chris Cuomo is the evil villain who brought down the laudable Jeff Zucker, instead of Donald Trump or any of the "deplorables" like Steve Bannon, Roger Stone, or Alex Jones.

Was this the end of the brief but bloody CNN civil war, with the casualties being the governor of New York, a CNN anchor, and a CNN president?

Or were there even more bombshells to drop?

***

It took only a day for the next salvos to be fired. On Thursday, February 3, 2022, the *Wall Street Journal* reported on some of the backstage machinations of this media drama:

> Days after he fired Mr. [Chris] Cuomo on a December Saturday—a termination that happened over the phone—Mr. Zucker told CNN employees that the network wouldn't pay Mr. Cuomo a severance, The Wall Street Journal reported at the time. He also said he had decided to fire Mr. Cuomo after he found out that the former anchor had been helping his brother

Andrew Cuomo to a greater degree than what Chris Cuomo had told CNN executives.

Cuomo hired lawyer Bryan Freedman, who contacted CNN to discuss severance Mr. Cuomo felt he was owed, the people said. During discussions with CNN about Mr. Cuomo's severance, Mr. Cuomo's legal team brought up examples of ways in which they believed the company had applied its policies inconsistently, including the case of Mr. Zucker and Ms. Gollust's relationship.[63]

The picture becomes a little clearer about how these media titans act behind closed doors. A firing over the telephone of a longtime employee, not a face-to-face discussion. Cuomo had been one of Zucker's first hires when he joined CNN in 2013.[64] This was loyalty?

Zucker was claiming in effect that he's not going to give one red cent to Cuomo, and Cuomo responds with claims of how other transgressions involving Zucker had been handled. CNN would have Americans believe these media people were the best among us. But the human resources manager of even the smallest company would know better than to this behave way.

And how might Chris Cuomo have possibly gotten the idea that it was acceptable to assist his brother, the governor of New York? Maybe because Jeff Zucker and Allison Gollust had done exactly the same thing? This is from the *New York Post* on February 3, 2022:

> Gollust and Zucker—the latter of whom dramatically quit CNN Wednesday after their affair was exposed— also gave Andrew Cuomo endless positive coverage because of their relationship, sources said.

> "While those 11:30 a.m. daily briefings by Andrew were across every network, they boosted ratings in a poorly performing slot for CNN," one source said.

According to a source to Cuomo, "Zucker and Gollust even advised Andrew what to say—how to respond and particularly how to hit back at [President Donald] Trump to make it more compelling TV."

"No network head should be coaching an elected official," the source added. "It's absolutely the antithesis of CNN's standards of business."[65]

If the story is to be believed, Jeff Zucker and Allison Gollust were essentially part of the New York State government (state-run media?) since they were advising Andrew Cuomo on his COVID press briefings. This seemed to be an inversion of the traditional standards of journalism, which is to hold authority accountable, not give advice to those same authorities on how to make a better presentation.

On the Sunday night edition of his show *Reliable Sources*, Brian Stelter addressed the situation and presented some historical background:

"This is the ugliest shakeup at CNN since the days Ted Turner was walking the halls," Stelter said, referring to the network's founder who was eventually forced out of the company....

The "background" to Zucker's exit, Stelter said, is the mega merger between Discovery and CNN's parent company WarnerMedia. The parties want the merger to go smoothly, Stelter argued, so Zucker and the controversies surrounding him had to be out of the way. Stelter said Zucker's departure probably wouldn't have occurred without the very public firing of anchor Chris Cuomo. In fact, the CNN host said one could "draw a straight line" from disgraced ex-New York Gov. Andrew Cuomo's downfall directly to Zucker's, saying it was "almost Shakespearean."[66]

While Chris Cuomo was busy lobbing bombshells at CNN, CNN was firing off some salvos of its own, accusing Cuomo of sexual harassment. As CNN's Stelter wrote in a later article:

> A few hours after CNN's announcement, the New York Times reported that a lawyer, Deborah Katz, had on Wednesday told CNN of an allegation of sexual misconduct made against Chris Cuomo by a client of hers.

> Katz did not immediately respond to a request for a comment. Neither did a spokesperson for Cuomo, though the spokesperson did comment to the Times, saying, "These apparently anonymous allegations are not true."

> A CNN spokesperson said in a statement, "Based on the report we received regarding Chris's conduct with his brother's defense, we had cause to terminate. When new allegations came to us this week, we took them seriously, and saw no reason to delay taking immediate action."[67]

Let's put this last article by Brian Stelter in its proper perspective. The people who knew Chris Cuomo the best, his employers at CNN, had no problem believing that the sexual misconduct allegations were likely to be true and chose to rid themselves of their most popular anchor, without any further discussion.

Although Ted Turner had publicly announced in 2018 that he was suffering from Lewy body dementia, one must wonder what he makes of what has become of his beloved network. (Cary and Kent requested an interview through Ted Turner's representative but received no answer.)

Even Don Lemon, who for years had engaged in banter with Chris Cuomo on the nightly handoff between their shows, seemed to turn on Cuomo as the scandal deepened. As reported by Fox News:

> Lemon turned on his old network pal on Monday [six days after Zucker's resignation] as WarnerMedia CEO Jason Kilar fielded questions during an in-house town hall from disgruntled CNN staffers who are depressed and angry that CNN's now-former boss, Jeff Zucker, was forced to step down last week.
>
> Kilar was reportedly asked if CNN will pay Cuomo his severance when Lemon jumped in.
>
> "Did you think about what message it sends to journalists in the company and also to the larger public that someone can be found to break with those journalistic standards and then get paid handsomely for it?" Lemon asked, according to the Wall Street Journal.
>
> Kilar didn't answer the question.[68]

It's important when doing an investigation such as the one described in this book to acknowledge when the subjects of one's inquiry do the right thing. Don Lemon is exactly right to pose such a question to the head of WarnerMedia, and people should praise Lemon for his actions.

In a rare move, the editorial board of the *New York Post* weighed in with its opinion of the ethics of CNN in this scandal:

> It was a seething nest of conflicts of interest that also included the gov's brother, CNN star Chris Cuomo, and Zucker's paramour, top CNN exec Allison Gollust— also a former communication director for Andrew.

The object of their collusion: To make Cuomo into a state and national savior figure…before the governor got taken down by his own alleged sexual misdeeds.

Zucker helped lead the public laundering of Cuomo's disastrous COVID policies, which saw the pandemic rip through New York as the governor piled restriction on useless restriction, closed schools and shoved elderly people with COVID into nursing homes (afterward hiding numbers on the deaths that resulted).[69]

While this was an opinion piece, it read as actual journalism. This was a fair reading of the scandal involving Governor Cuomo and CNN. CNN had violated the rules of journalism and, yet even when caught, didn't miss a beat and quickly got to work constructing a narrative that didn't make it look so bad.

So here we are. Zucker did nothing wrong, his ouster says, by violating the public trust still placed (we don't know why) in CNN. He did nothing wrong by cozying up to the powerful and setting up a revolving door between government and the media.

He did nothing wrong by breaking every rule of journalistic ethics and allowing a governor to be interviewed by his own brother, with no challenges to the terrible policies he had put in place.

He did nothing wrong by making an epochal crisis for New York that much worse.

No. What he did wrong was engaging in *legal* bedroom antics.

And this deranged narrative about Zucker looks like it's going to win.[70]

However, the *New York Post* may have been too pessimistic. Recent evidence suggests that even if Zucker escapes this scandal with some shred of dignity, the public seems to be turning away from CNN. One wonders if former viewers of CNN are simply finding better things to do with their time.

Perhaps they cannot be convinced to denounce their once-beloved network but, like many of us when we discover we've been in an unhealthy relationship, quietly move on and resolve to do better next time. A December 2021 Daily Beast article pointed out the hard times upon which CNN had fallen:

> At the beginning of 2021, CNN was on top of the cable world.
>
> The network, which revolutionized round-the-clock news coverage when it launched more than four decades ago, had finally retaken the ratings crown from Fox News and pushed its conservative rival to third place for the first time since 2000.
>
> Less than a year later, CNN's viewership has sunk— the channel is buried in third place behind Fox and MSNBC after a series of controversies and scandals that ostensibly struck a blow to the news network's credibility.
>
> In fact, just this past week the network averaged a paltry 585,000 total viewers in primetime, placing CNN all the way back in 17th place among all basic cable.[71]

The United States is home to more than 325 million people. These trends do not look encouraging, although to be fair, much of the news media is experiencing a downward trend in viewership. Is this because many of them have adopted a similar "fear and isolation" strategy against opposing viewpoints, and after a period, people simply become too exhausted to live in a constant state of terror?

People are social creatures by nature, living for hundreds of thousands of years in relatively small tribes numbering fewer than a hundred people; then came towns and cities, nation-states, the global community, and yet in many ways humans are more isolated from each other than when they lived in those small tribes. How many people does one need to interact with on a daily basis in order to feel connected to the rest of humanity? Fifteen? Twenty?

The faceless merchants of marketing have manipulated our psychology so that we are estranged from each other by the thoughts in our head. When we meet people, we perform a mental calculus: friend or foe? However, the vast majority of people are just trying to do their best to get by, hoping to contribute something to society and wanting the affection of others.

The tribe of genuinely good people is much larger than the tribe of genuinely bad people, and that is the optimistic view we should have when we interact with the world.

*** 

Although it will probably not be the last revelation, on February 16, 2022, Jeff Zucker's lover, Allison Gollust, resigned from CNN after an investigation into the spiraling scandal. WarnerMedia CEO Jason Kilar put out a statement:

> Based on interviews with more than 40 individuals and a review of over 100,000 texts and emails, the investigation found violations of Company policies, including CNN's News Standards and Practices, by Jeff Zucker, Allison Gollust, and Chris Cuomo.

> We have the highest standards of journalistic integrity at CNN, and those rules must apply to everyone equally. Given the information provided to me in the investigation, I strongly believe we have taken the right actions and the right decisions have been made.[72]

Are we to genuinely believe that CNN management was unaware of these problems? Or does CNN need to be cleaned up before the big merger with Discovery, slated for the summer of 2022? It's interesting that in a media outlet, it seems like people can't get their stories straight. In the wake of Kilar's statement, Allison Gollust put out her own statement:

> WarnerMedia's statement tonight is an attempt to retaliate against me and change the media narrative in the wake of their disastrous handling of the last two weeks. It is deeply disappointing that after spending the past nine years defending and upholding CNN's highest standards of journalistic integrity, I would be treated this way as I leave. But I do so with my head held high, knowing that I gave my heart and soul to working with the finest journalists in the world.[73]

The expression "these people deserve each other" comes to mind. How is it that, in a controversy involving four people, there are essentially five different versions of the truth?

It sounds like somebody could use a "fact-checker."

\*\*\*

What does the future hold for CNN?

Even before the resignations of Governor Cuomo, Chris Cuomo, Jeff Zucker, and Allison Gollust there were warning signs that the network might be radically different in the future.

On November 18, 2021, billionaire John Malone was interviewed about the upcoming merger of WarnerMedia and Discovery. As the deal was explained in a CNBC article:

> Back in May [2021], AT&T announced a deal to combine its content under WarnerMedia with Discovery. Under the agreement, AT&T will unwind its $85 billion acquisition of TimeWarner, which closed just three years ago and form a new and separate media company with Discovery.... At the time of the announcement, the parties had said they hoped to close the transaction in the middle of next year [summer 2022].[74]

It is not anyone's fault that media organizations have become just another commodity to be traded on the market, like soybeans or pork belly futures. But maybe there are investors with long-term visions of the health of their holdings, the way a farmer wants to make sure that his land remains healthy for future generations. There may even be reason to hope for a badly compromised news network like CNN if radical changes are made. These discussions already seem to be taking place.

> There's a place for CNN in the proposed $43 billion combination of WarnerMedia and Discovery, billionaire media mogul John Malone told CNBC in a recorded interview that aired Thursday.
>
> "I would like to see CNN evolve back to the kind of journalism that it started with, and actually have journalists, which would be unique and refreshing," said the cable TV pioneer and longtime chairman of Liberty Media, which is a major shareholder in Discovery. "I do believe good journalism could have a role in this future portfolio that Discovery-TimeWarner's going to represent."[75]

You might reasonably ask how Cary, a CNN whistleblower, feels about these comments by one of the new owners of CNN.

It fills him with an enormous sense of satisfaction—as if the troubles, doubts, and sleepless nights were worth it. Cary suffered greatly during that time, wracked with guilt, and doubt about whether he was doing the right thing. There was the organization, CNN, which was doing bad things, and yet there were people with jobs who were just trying to put food on the table, send their kids to college, and hoping to maybe find a few pleasurable hours each week with family and friends.

However, with the news about Zucker, Cary is hopeful that many of these former CNN employees will now see what he did in a more favorable light. In a meeting with CNN employees the day after Zucker's resignation, CNN employees started to ask questions:

> WarnerMedia Chief Executive Jason Kilar was subject to intense criticism during a meeting with CNN employees Wednesday evening, where he was grilled over his decision that CNN President Jeff Zucker should step down after Mr. Kilar learned the network boss had a romantic relationship with CNN's marketing chief.
>
> During an hourlong meeting with Mr. Kilar, CNN anchors and employees expressed frustration that Mr. Zucker didn't get a second chance after disclosing the relationship with Allison Gollust and asked Mr. Kilar why Mr. Zucker was replaced abruptly. Mr. Kilar declined to answer questions about the timeline of Mr. Zucker's departure, though he said that he followed a process "with an appropriate sense of urgency."[76]

The meeting between CNN employees and WarnerMedia CEO Jason Kilar did not go well. That's often what happens when one gives unsatisfying answers, as any police detective can attest. A story needs to make sense, or it isn't believable. A hint of what might have prompted the quick firing of Jeff Zucker over what seems to be a minor transgression was provided in an exchange with CNN anchor Jake Tapper and some CNN executives:

> During the question-and-answer session, anchor Jake Tapper said that former CNN host Chris Cuomo hired a lawyer who seemed eager to leak damaging information about Mr. Zucker unless they gave Mr. Cuomo severance.
>
> "An outside observer might say, 'Well, it looks like Chris Cuomo succeeded,'" Mr. Tapper said. "He threatened Jeff. Jeff said we don't negotiate with terrorists. And Chris blew the place up. How do we get past that perception that this is the bad guy winning?"[77]

In some ways this exchange was more like something from *The Real Housewives of Beverly Hills* than "the most trusted name in news." Let's consider the insanity quotient of that last passage. One CNN host is calling a former CNN host a "terrorist." It's genuinely difficult to regain one's credibility after making such a statement.

In the wake of Zucker's departure, CNN seemed to be collapsing like a dysfunctional family in which one member decides to finally start airing the dirty laundry. It seems as if the resignation of Zucker was an attempt to staunch the bleeding, not just about the affair with Gollust but other, much more damaging revelations.

In the glare of the public spotlight, there were more secrets about to surface about CNN.

# CHAPTER FOUR

# Trump Damage, COVID Hysteria, and a Story CNN Should Have Been Pursuing

Project Veritas continued releasing stories dealing with CNN and consulting Cary on background to better understand the videos it was receiving.

On April 13, 2021, Project Veritas released Part 1 of a new investigation of CNN, featuring CNN technical director Charlie Chester. By that time, Donald Trump had lost the 2020 presidential election, and President Joe Biden had been inaugurated. Charlie Chester claimed that CNN was responsible for Trump's loss and that he came to work for the network specifically for that purpose. In addition, he also talked about how CNN manipulates its viewers, why the COVID-19 crisis was great for ratings, and how CNN tries to hide the radical agenda of the official Black Lives Matter movement.

The video opened with James O'Keefe reporting from the lobby of CNN's New York office. Yes, James likes to push a few buttons.

> JAMES O'KEEFE: I'm standing here at 30 Hudson Yards, WarnerMedia is right there [points]. That's CNN's corporate headquarters. We're in New York City. Jim Sciutto [CNN's chief national security correspondent and co-anchor of *Newsroom*] just walked out. Funny enough, I asked him about the videos we have just obtained of a CNN director, Charlie Chester, on tape. [Footage of Sciutto being asked questions by O'Keefe and not answering.]
>
> For years we've heard that CNN is the most trusted name in news. But a CNN director is on tape, telling us that it's propaganda, helping a certain political candidate. Employees admitting what we've always known to be true. This time, it's on tape.
>
> [Video shifts to show undercover video of Charlie Chester at a restaurant.]
>
> CHARLIE CHESTER: Look what we did. We [CNN] got Trump out. I am a hundred percent going to say it. And I a hundred percent believe it. If it wasn't for CNN, I don't know that Trump would have got voted out. I really don't think so.[78]

A CNN employee, "a hundred percent" believes that his network was responsible for Trump's loss in the 2020 election. He joins many conservatives who believe the exact same thing. And as an example of how CNN managed to do that, Chester details CNN's fake story that Trump must be neurologically damaged and how the network brought in a parade of what can only be assumed to be left-wing medical "experts" to make the same argument. How is it possible that a news network is willingly engaging in such behavior? And how is it, when Project Veritas releases this information, that nothing of any consequence seems to happen to the people responsible?

Chester was then asked a question by an undercover Project Veritas journalist:

> PROJECT VERITAS JOURNALIST: I guess I have a confession. I worry about Biden and his health, I guess.

> CHARLIE CHESTER: Your news health?

> PROJECT VERITAS JOURNALIST: What? No, I said Biden, our President. Like I want to just, like, literally—

> CHESTER: Oh, his health?

> PROJECT VERITAS JOURNALIST: I just want to, like take care of him, and make sure he's okay.

> CHESTER: He is definitely, the whole thing of him running during the entire, like, for the campaign, showing him jogging, was obviously deflection. Obviously, because of his age and they're trying to make it like, "Oh, I'm healthy."[79]

Chester was clear in this vignette that CNN was actively trying to allay the fears of voters that Biden wasn't physically up for the job. Charlie Chester's dad was worried that Biden would die in office, a fear not shared by his son. But even if Biden did die, Chester is not worried about the prospect of a Kamala Harris presidency.

However, CNN wasn't done propping up Joe Biden. The help continued into his presidency, as revealed by additional footage talking about when Biden tripped up a flight of stairs.

> CHARLIE CHESTER: Did we harp on Trump tripping? I think we talked about it a little bit. As long as we talk about it a little bit with Biden, I think we're golden.

> RACHELLE HOFFMAN, CNN Graphics Producer: But, like, we didn't cover it at all on Don [Lemon]. Like, we didn't talk about it. Whereas if it had been Trump tripping up the stairs—

> JAMES O'KEEFE: Chester didn't just take credit for Trump's loss. He alleges it was CNN's "focus." They were focused on getting Trump out of office. Chester also believes in the current news cycle, there is "COVID fatigue," Chester saying that CNN has a game plan to fix that fatigue.

> CHESTER: I think there's just like a COVID fatigue, So. Like whenever a new story comes up, they're going to latch onto it. They've already announced in our office that once the public is open to it, we're going to be, our next, I don't know what's the word I'm looking for? I don't know, like it's going to be our focus. Our focus was to get Trump out of office, right? Without saying it, that's what it was, right?

> So, our next thing is going to be climate change awareness.[80]

It doesn't get much clearer. Two older presidents exhibit some typical problems associated with age. In one case, there appears to be a trembling hand. Since it's Trump's, that requires an army of medical experts expressing the opinion that he's lost it.

In the other case, Biden trips going up a flight of stairs. Mention is made of it, but no similar medical panel is convened to suggest a similar loss of mental capacity.

In addition to CNN's anti-Trump jihad, the network keeps riding its COVID fear warhorse, and when that peters out, it's got the next crisis to terrify you: climate change.

> PROJECT VERITAS JOURNALIST: What does that look like?
>
> CHARLIE CHESTER: I don't know. I'm not sure. I have a feeling it's just going to be like constantly showing videos of like decline in ice and weather warming up and the effects it's having on the economy. And really tapping into that.
>
> PROJECT VERITAS JOURNALIST: Who decides that?
>
> CHESTER: The head of the network.
>
> PROJECT VERITAS JOURNALIST: Who is that? Is that Zucker?
>
> CHESTER: Zucker, yeah. I imagine that he's got his counsel and they've all discussed where they think—
>
> PROJECT VERITAS JOURNALIST: So, that's like the next—
>
> CHESTER: Pandemic-like story, that we'll beat to death. But that one's got longevity. You know what I mean? It's not like, is it, definitive ending to the pandemic, or you know, like, it'll taper off to a point that

it's not a problem anymore. Climate change is gonna take years. So, they'll probably be able to milk that for quite a bit.

PROJECT VERITAS JOURNALIST: So, climate change overload?

CHESTER: Stories, like right now, we have an inside track right now. Where two stories are going to get pushed. Climate change is going to be the next COVID thing for CNN. We're going to home in on it.

RACHELLE HOFFMAN, CNN Graphics Producer: Focus on that.

CHESTER: I love it. [Sarcastic.]

HOFFMAN: But that's a fair thing to focus on.

CHESTER: But to commit to that as a network?

PROJECT VERITAS JOURNALIST: You said it's going to be like the new COVID?

CHESTER: I'm feeling, well, that's the way it was billed. Unless that was just a call to arms to get people to start writing, and then we'll assess it. I don't know, but—

PROJECT VERITAS JOURNALIST: Do you think it's just going to be like a lot of fear for the climate?

CHESTER: Yeah. Fear sells.[81]

In Charlie Chester's opinion, CNN wasn't bringing people the news, it was creating a world filled with fear. First, there was the Trump fear, then the COVID fear, and in the future we're going to be subjected to fear of the climate crisis. This can only be considered an extraordinary betrayal of the vision of CNN founder Ted Turner, who wanted to bring people closer together with information they might not normally receive.

According to Chester, the blame for this situation rested squarely with CNN president Jeff Zucker.

In the next video released by Project Veritas, Chester would detail exactly the methods used by CNN to terrify its viewers.

\*\*\*

One of the questions conservatives often ask about our adversaries is whether they genuinely understand the damage they are causing. It's one thing for conservatives to accuse members of the mainstream media of bias. But what's really going on in the mind of one of those members?

In their personal opinion, are they being fair, or are they aware of the hypocrisy?

For Charlie Chester, the answer seems to be clear, as he details exactly how guests and viewers are manipulated. But there was another overwhelming sense that Cary got as he watched the video. Chester seemed genuinely troubled by what CNN was doing and by his own role in those actions.

Although it's not certain, it wouldn't be surprising if in some small part of his soul, Chester was happy to have his thoughts broadcast to the world in a Project Veritas release. He came across to Cary as somewhat of a broken man in a fallen world, an idealist who'd seen behind the curtain, and doubted that there might be any truly good place left in the media landscape. O'Keefe set the stage for viewers, again reporting from the lobby of WarnerMedia in New York City:

CHARLIE CHESTER: It's fear. Like fear, really drives numbers [TV ratings]. It does, you know. The happiest days in news, people, I would imagine, turn it off and then they go with their family. They don't stay glued to it unless there's something that's uniting them like a moon landing or something like that. Fear is the thing that keeps you tuned in, I would imagine. What's the scariest thing next, you know?

[The video cuts to a different shot of Chester.]

CHESTER: Sad news doesn't do well with ratings. You know, like, if you can get someone impassioned, that really does well with ratings. Sad news, back to back to back, doesn't really do well, unless it affects them directly. COVID? Gangbusters with ratings, right? Which is why we constantly have the death toll on the side.

Which, I have a major problem with how we're tallying how many people die every day. Because I've even looked at it and been like, let's make it higher. Like why isn't it high enough, you know, today?

And I'm like, what the fuck am I rallying for? That's a problem that we're doing that, you know?

PROJECT VERITAS JOURNALIST: Well, I mean, it helps with ratings.

CHESTER: Of course, yeah. But, yeah, at what expense? I have a job. Sure. Like, I'm happy about that. But, I don't know.

PROJECT VERITAS JOURNALIST: Who gets to decide how long that stays on?

CHESTER: Head of the network. I've been in the room many a times when my director tells me to take it down. And I take it down. And then we get a phone call, like the Bat-phone rings in the back. Literally, a red phone. Like the special red phone rings and they pick it up. And the producer picks it up. And you hear murmur, murmur, murmur and every so often they put it on speaker and it's like the head of the network being like, "There's nothing that you're doing right now that makes me want to stick. Put the numbers back up because that's the most enticing thing we had. So, put it back up." So, like things like that are constantly talked about.

RACHELLE HOFFMAN, CNN Graphics Producer: It's most likely a Jeff Zucker call.[82]

Charlie Chester talks about how he often found himself urging the COVID death totals to go higher, only to realize the sickness of this behavior. And while others at CNN were disturbed, like his director, their effort to marginally lower the hysteria of the country by taking down the graphic was quickly countermanded by Jeff Zucker calling on the red Bat-phone in the back of the office.

Is this really the way CNN was being run?

One thinks back to the golden days of journalism in the 1970s, when reporters from the *Washington Post* were convincing their editor to publish the Pentagon Papers, revealing the government's lies about the Vietnam War, or the Watergate scandal, which brought down President Richard Nixon. That was journalism. They were investigations led by journalists, following their instincts, hunches, and information, not some network president calling and saying, "There's nothing you're doing now that makes me want to stick."

PROJECT VERITAS JOURNALIST: Why don't you guys at CNN show the recovery rates on the death tolls, at least?

CHARLIE CHESTER: Recovery rates? Oh, who's had it and then—

PROJECT VERITAS JOURNALIST: Recovered.

CHESTER: Because that's not scary. I would imagine that's why they don't do it. Yeah.

PROJECT VERITAS JOURNALIST: That's what I figured.

CHESTER: If it bleeds, it leads.

PROJECT VERITAS JOURNALIST: If it bleeds, it leads. I like that.

CHESTER: I think no one ever says these things out loud. But it's obvious, based on the number of the stories that we do. Like the fact that we have a segment called "The Good Stuff," which is a feel-good thing. But it's a dedicated moment at the end, to like, almost like the ice cream to alleviate, you know, everything that you've been through. Like something sweet to end it with, cause everything else is like doom and gloom.

I mean, it's human nature. I find myself watching more
news when there's something looming and scary.[83]

If there's a pandemic, it stands to reason that, just as one would
want to know the death rate, one would also want to know the recovery rate, of those who did nothing and of those who might have
been treated with hydroxychloroquine or ivermectin. After all, this
is a "novel" virus, so it may require "novel" solutions. That's just
common sense.

Chester also seems to be very glum about how human nature
stays glued to news about terrible things, rather than happy things.
It's really a perverse incentive. Bad news gets ratings, while good
news doesn't. However, the danger, like the classic story of the boy
who cried wolf, lies in what happens when you constantly claim the
world is ending, and yet somehow the world survives. After the third
supposed Armageddon, it's more difficult to believe in the next end-
of-the-world scenario. Chester explained how to terrify a population.

> CHARLIE CHESTER: Any reporter on CNN. What
> they're actually doing is they're telling the person
> what to say. It's an art form in there. There's an art
> form to it. But it would be like the accident thing you
> just saw. [The Project Veritas journalist had appar-
> ently witnessed a car accident earlier in the evening
> where a motorist blew through an intersection and hit
> another car.]
>
> One of the reporters would be like, so, then you know,
> that man clearly went through the intersection, slam-
> ming into the car. And you know, it really is unfortu-
> nate that, you know, our infrastructure of traffic lights
> and whatnot, is falling apart in the city. How do you
> feel about the traffic lights and the infrastructure?

We've led them to talk about how we want them to talk about it. It's always like leading them in a direction before they even open their mouths. And the only people that we will let on the air, for the most part, are people that have a proven track record of taking the bait.

I think there's an art to manipulation. I think some people have figured it out inherently.

PROJECT VERITAS JOURNALIST: Like in the media, or just like in general?

CHESTER: Media. And just in conversation.

PROJECT VERITAS JOURNALIST: Yeah, yeah, yeah.

CHESTER: I think, when, like, you ever meet somebody that you feel you're being gaslit by? Start to listen to how they word things.

PROJECT VERITAS JOURNALIST: What do you mean?

CHESTER: Inflection, saying things like twice. There's little subtleties to how to manipulate people.[84]

Cary wishes he could get angry at Charlie Chester for his comments. But he appears sad and pathetic, a hollow man, a soulless drone marching off to work every day to collect a paycheck for a job in which he no longer believes.

And yet, aren't people like Charlie Chester uniquely dangerous to society? He knows that what he's doing is wrong, he sees the hypocrisy, and even acknowledges that, from a certain point of view, he's one of the "bad guys." Journalists are supposed to be like umpires in a baseball game, calling balls and strikes. Our very system of government is based on trusting the media, not believing that journalists are getting their marching orders from the network president. But Chester continues soldiering on for that paycheck, fully aware of the damage his news network is doing to the country. He does not take action to right a wrong.

That is the ultimate definition of cowardice.

How can any decent person be part of such an organization?

Cary will wait for anyone to provide him with an answer.

***

The last video is relatively brief, but quickly gets to the point.

> CHARLIE CHESTER: I was trying to do some research on, like, the Asian hate. The people that are getting attacked and whatnot. A bunch of black men have been attacking Asians. I'm like, "What are you doing?" Like, we're [CNN] trying to like help with the BLM [Black Lives Matter] and you're going to like? I mean, it's individuals. It's not a people, you know? It's not good. The optics of that are not good.

> The little things like that are enough to set back movements. Because the far Left will start to latch on and create a story of like criminalizing an entire people. You know, just easier headlines that way, I guess. Yeah, I don't know.

> PROJECT VERITAS JOURNALIST: So, you're saying that the far Left would label a whole genre [group] of people? I kind of missed your point.

> CHESTER: No, the conservatives. I'm sorry. Not the far Left. I've noticed that you'll get headlines that,

you know, might lump people together as opposed to focusing on the individual. I mean, that's what Trump ended up doing with like the "China virus" and that puts so much blame on an entire group of people, as opposed to, you know, a few careless people.

PROJECT VERITAS JOURNALIST: Right. Right. The actual source, right?

CHESTER: Yeah, yeah.

PROJECT VERITAS JOURNALIST: I mean, but is it normal for the media to like, so say there's a white shooter [or] black shooter? Which one are we going to, you know, like—

CHESTER: Yeah, for the longest while, the story was like, people were lapping up that it was like, you know, white guys for so long. I don't, I haven't seen anything focusing on the color of people's skin that aren't white. They're just not, all of a sudden, that story loses a little steam from it. They just like leave it be.

PROJECT VERITAS JOURNALIST: Why?

CHESTER: I don't know. I think it's gotta be trends, what people will latch onto, you know?[85]

The Left's choice of words is important. Traditionally, Americans would talk about the "public square," an idealized version of Colonial America where everybody was free to speak his mind. But apparently, the "public square" ideal is far too democratic for CNN and other members of the mainstream media. That would seem to imply that there is something called "free speech" to which every person was somehow entitled as a beloved child of God.

It's much more restrictive to talk about a "platform" on which only the elite are allowed to ascend and speak to the citizenry. Or in the parlance of Charlie Chester, those who "take the bait" that the CNN hosts dangle in front of them with their biased questions. It's not too much of a leap to say that CNN, and any other media who follow this practice, is profoundly undemocratic. O'Keefe ended the segment with these words:

> JAMES O'KEEFE: Is CNN the most trusted name in news? Their own employees are telling us that they're not. But the same employees that tell us they're not, are also participating in the propaganda they're ashamed of. And that's perhaps the greatest tragedy of all.... Stand by the credo of journalism; inform the people. You have an obligation and a duty to the people, without fear or favor. I doubt Charlie Chester will be the last employee we hear from at CNN. Stay tuned, America.[86]

Project Veritas had done a remarkable investigative job going after CNN for its bias. Prior to Cary's involvement, Project Veritas had gotten CNN commentator Van Jones saying on video that the Russia collusion story was a "nothing burger." Then with Cary's undercover video documenting rampant anti-Trump bias, and with the Charlie Chester release, Project Veritas had shown that CNN took credit for Trump's 2020 loss; that CNN wanted to keep people in a state of fear about COVID, and when that faded, CNN would be ready to promote climate hysteria; and that if stories arose that questioned the narrative of Black Lives Matter, CNN wouldn't pursue them.

In light of these facts, it's hard to describe CNN as a news organization anymore.

***

If CNN is no longer a news organization, what is it?

James O'Keefe is fond of quoting the late-nineteenth-century humorist Finley Peter Dunne that "the job of a newspaper is to afflict the comfortable and comfort the afflicted." With CNN engaging in all these acts of bias, was any time left for genuine investigative reporting? James is also fond of William Randolph Hearst's declaration that "news is something somebody doesn't want printed; all the rest is advertisement."

The world was "afflicted" in 2020 by the COVID-19 crisis, and if there was ever an opportunity for genuine investigative reporting, it was with the origins of this virus. Did CNN do any actual, probing investigations, coming to conclusions that might have been at odds with those in charge of public health?

No, it did not. A typical CNN story during this time was published by CNN editor-at-large Chris Cillizza on May 5, 2020, just a little over a month and a half after the nationwide lockdowns began. The title of the article was "Anthony Fauci Just Crushed Donald Trump's Theory on the Origins of the Coronavirus." Here's how it opened:

> For weeks now, President Donald Trump has been making the case that the coronavirus originated not in nature but in a lab in Wuhan, China. He said late last week that he had a "high degree of confidence" that was what happened (although he didn't specify why he felt that way) and on Sunday night in a Fox town hall had offered cryptically "something happened."
>
> Enter Anthony Fauci, the head of the National Institute of Allergy and Infectious Disease and perhaps the single most prominent doctor in the world at the moment. In an interview with National Geographic posted on Monday night, Fauci was definitive about the origins of the virus which has sickened more than a million Americans and killed more than 68,000:

"If you look at the evolution of the virus in bats and what's out there now, [the scientific evidence] is very, very strongly leaning toward this could not have been artificially or deliberately manipulated.... Everything about the stepwise evolution over time strongly indicates that [this virus] evolved in nature and then jumped species."[87]

Is it clear how CNN was manipulating the public during this time? The United States president, whom one can assume to be the best-informed person in the government, as well as having a world-class bullshit detector, was coming to the conclusion that this virus had escaped from a Chinese lab.

Without providing any evidence for review, Dr. Fauci was expressing a different opinion, and CNN quickly and unquestioningly took his side. But perhaps CNN should not be subjected to such harsh criticism, especially as this was the view it was also being fed by the intelligence community. Cillizza continued:

In short, Fauci's view on the origins of the disease matters a whole lot more than Trump's opinion about where it came from. Especially because, outside of Trump and his immediate inner circle, most people in a position to know are very, very skeptical of the Trump narrative that the virus came out of a lab—whether accidentally or on purpose.

Like the intelligence community, which in a statement last week via the Office of the Director of National Intelligence said this: "The Intelligence Community also concurs with the wide scientific consensus that the COVID-19 virus was not manmade or genetically modified."[88]

Did CNN think to question whether Dr. Fauci might have any conflicts of interest regarding his opinion on the COVID-19 virus? Might there be any reason to be skeptical of the intelligence agencies regarding their determination that the virus came from nature, rather than a lab? If so, CNN kept such thoughts to itself and did not share them with its viewers.

What might an investigation into such a question look like?

On January 10, 2022, Project Veritas released a report on several internal government documents that had been provided to it by a whistleblower, detailing our own government's response to proposed "gain of function" research on bat corona viruses.[89]

Kent Heckenlively, a lawyer, often advises Cary not to jump to conclusions but to wait for the evidence to come to him. Kent is fond of saying, "Don't try to guess what happened. You often can't imagine what kind of stupid shit people were doing until somebody who was actually there tells you. Be open to new information."

On January 19, 2018, the Defense Advanced Research Projects Agency (DARPA) released a "Broad Agency Announcement" about "PREventing EMerging Pathogenic Threats (PREEMPT),"[90] which asked for proposals on how to deal with emerging biological threats.

A group called the EcoHealth Alliance submitted a proposal. The following is from the executive summary of the March 24, 2018, proposal by the EcoHealth Alliance's Dr. Peter Daszak, under the subheading "Impact":

- Security concerns across Asia make the region a potential deployment site for US warfighters. Troops face increased disease risks from SARSr-CoVs, which are shed via urine and feces as bats forage at night.
- Our [The EcoHealth Alliance's] work in Yunan, China shows that: 1) bat SARSr-CoVs exist that can infect human cells, produce SARS-like illness in humanized mice, and are not affected by monoclonal or vaccine treatments; and 2) bat SARSr-CoV host-jump into local human populations

is frequent. These viruses are therefore a clear and present danger to US defense forces in the region and global health security.

- Our goal is to analyze, predict, then "DEFUSE" the spillover potential of novel bat-origin high risk SARSr-CoVs in Southeast Asia and across the virus's distribution. This will safeguard the US warfighter, reduce risk for local communities and their livestock, improving food and global health security.

- Our strategy is based on immune parameters that are found across all bat genomic groups. If successful, the DEFUSE approach can be adapted to other MERS-CoV in the Middle East, other SARSr-CoVs in Africa, and other bat-origin viruses (e.g. Hendra, Nipah, Ebola, Marburg viruses.)[91]

In detailing the cost of the plan, Daszak noted that phase one would cost $8,411,546, and phase two would cost $5,797,699, for a total cost of $14,209,245.[92]

The executive summary paints a relatively clear picture of the plan: identify potentially harmful bat corona viruses, predict their evolution by genetically manipulating them in humanized mice (mice that have had genetic modifications such that their immune system mimics that of a human being), then create vaccines that are then sprayed onto or breathed in by the bats in their caves.

And all this was being done so that if US troops needed to invade China, or someplace else in Asia, they wouldn't contract these rare viruses. (Yes, it sounds like a plan from a James Bond or Austin Powers movie.) What makes even less sense is that EcoHealth Alliance and DARPA were getting help from Chinese scientists in the research. One day, you're working with the Chinese, the next day you're invading their country and hoping the local bats don't give you a disease when they urinate on you.

It could happen.

The next section of the executive summary detailed which interventions would take place if this plan was approved:

(1) Broadscale immune boosting: Inoculate bats with immune modulators to upregulate their naturally-inhibited immunity and suppress viral replication, transiently reducing viral shedding/spillover risk.

(2) Targeted immune boosting: In concert with above, inoculate bats with novel chimeric polyvalent recombinant spike proteins to enhance their adaptive immune memory against specific, high risk viruses.

Viral dynamics: Develop stochastic simulation models to estimate the frequency, efficacy, and population coverage required for intervention approaches to effectively suppress the viral population.

Field trial: Use team expertise in wildlife vaccine delivery (transdermal nanoparticles, racoon poxvirus vector) to develop effective molecule delivery via automated aerosolization onto bats at roost entrance at our three test cave sites in a cave complex in Yunnan, China, where SARSr-CoVs have infected people.[93]

The researchers had come up with a plan that bordered on insanity, like something out of a Michael Crichton novel where scientists think it's a good idea to resurrect dinosaurs. However, in this demented fantasy they're creating viral monsters that never existed in the past, and might not exist in the future.

Miners in China had come down with a coronavirus infection from bats in the mines in which they worked. Rather than giving them better protection, or possibly keeping the mines clear of bats, an elaborate plan was created by EcoHealth Alliance and Peter Daszak. Instead of avoiding these bats (or minimizing the ill effects of contact), scientists would seek out these bats and give them immune boosters, and then eventually they'd give the bats these "novel chimeric polyvalent recombinant spike proteins."

We probably need to break these words down.

"Novel" means new, never before seen in nature.

"Chimeric" means composed of parts from several different species, such as in this case, bats, mice, humans, and—it seems we've also added a racoon to the mixture.

"Polyvalent" means providing protection against many different microorganisms.

"Recombinant" means created from several different species (the aforementioned bats, mice, humans, and racoon), and "spike proteins" are the jagged protuberances from a virus (which look like spikes) that puncture the cell and allow the virus to inject its viral DNA so that the cell can become a virus production facility.

You might know "novel chimeric polyvalent spike proteins" by another name: mRNA vaccines. Yes, the kind produced by Pfizer and Moderna to lessen the effects of COVID-19.

*\*\**

The forty-four-page proposal submitted by the EcoHealth Alliance on March 24, 2018, contained detailed information on its plans for bat coronaviruses—and, if an organization such as CNN or the *New York Times* had reported on the information, public opinion about the true heroes and villains of this epidemic might have been vastly different.

The research was to be conducted in two stages, as described in section II of the EcoHealth Alliance proposal:

> Our goal is to defuse the potential for spillover of novel bat-origin high-zoonotic risk SARS-related coronaviruses in Asia. In **TA1** we will intensively sample bats at our field sites where we have identified high spillover risk SARSr-CoVs. We will sequence their spike proteins, reverse engineer them to conduct binding assays, and insert them into bat SARSr-CoV (WIV1, SCHO14) backbones (these use bat-SARSr-CoV backbones, not SARS-CoV, and are exempt from

dual-use and gain of function concerns) to infect humanized mice and assess capacity to cause SARS-like disease. Our modeling team will use these data to build **machine-learning genotype-phenotype models** of viral evolution and spillover risk.[94]

This should be the "smoking gun" as to whether there was genetic manipulation of bat corona viruses before the outbreak of COVID-19. However, since those in charge get to define what is and what is not "gain of function," they simply define it away. (Cary also notes his coauthor Kent's concern detailed in many of his previous books that the mixing of animal and human tissues in either the creation of these new organisms or in vaccine production creates a high risk of viral spillover from the animals into humans, where they may cause disease.) Whenever Cary reads the phrase "humanized mice," it strikes him as fundamentally wrong. The label "mice people" just makes so much more sense, but maybe that's just Cary's bias.

Regardless of the nomenclature, the greater concern is that scientists were taking these bat viruses and making them infectious in mice, which were genetically designed so that their immune system would be similar to that of humans. This means that if these newly designed viruses can infect "humanized mice," they can also affect humans. Many question whether that's exactly what happened, and the failure of our health authorities to address this question only further heightens the suspicions of the public. The proposal continued:

> We will uniquely validate these with serology from previously collected human samples via LIPS assays that assess which spike proteins allow spillover into people. We will build **host-pathogen spatial models** to predict the bat species composition of caves across Southeast Asia, parameterized with a full inventory of host-virus distribution at our field test sites, three caves in Yunan Province, China, and a series of unique

global datasets on bat-host viral relationships. By the end of Y1, we will create a prototype app for the warfighter that identifies the likelihood of bats harboring dangerous viral pathogens at any site across Asia.[95]

Does anybody else find it curious that Dr. Peter Daszak of the EcoHealth Alliance was interested in creating a "prototype app for the warfighter that identifies the likelihood of bats harboring dangerous viral pathogens at any site across Asia"? When you hear of an organization called EcoHealth Alliance, don't you envision harp seals in Canada being saved from hunters, or elephants being protected from poachers in Africa?

But an app for the American warfighter in Asia to be protected from rare bat viruses?

We don't know about you, but that sounds like some serious CIA shit to us.

The document continued with the blueprint for Daszak's plan:

In **TA2**, we will evaluate two approaches to SARSr-CoV shedding in cave bats: (1) **Broadscale immune boosting**, in which we will inoculate bats with immune modulators to upregulate their innate immune response and downregulate viral replication; (2) Targeted immune boosting, in which we will inoculate bats with novel chimeric polyvalent recombinant spike proteins plus the immune modulator to enhance immunity against specific, high-risk viruses. We will trial inoculum delivery methods on captive bats including a novel automated aerosolization system, transdermal nanoparticle application and edible adhesive gels.... The most effective biologicals will be trialed in our test cave sits in Yunan Province, with reduction in viral shedding as proof of concept.[96]

This plan envisioned some sort of facility where there would be "captive bats" upon which scientists could experiment? The likely location of this lab? Not in America. Not in Yunan Province.

Instead, it would be located hundreds of miles away at China's only Bio-Safety Level 4 lab, the Wuhan Institute of Virology.

\*\*\*

The organization to which Dr. Peter Daszak and the EcoHealth Alliance submitted their proposal is DARPA.

What is DARPA?

It depends on your perspective.

It either consists of the scariest group of people you've never heard of, or it's the vanguard of our freedom, making sure that we have technological capabilities far greater than any of our potential adversaries. Here is one account of its founding from a 2004 *Mother Jones* article:

> When, in October 1957, the USSR launched the first manmade earth satellite, the basketball-sized Sputnik, it caught the United States off guard and sent the government into fits. Not only had the Soviets exploded an atomic bomb years before the Americans had predicted they would, but now they were leading the "space race." In response, the Defense Department approved funding for a new U.S. satellite project, headed by former Nazi SS Officer Wernher von Braun, and created, in 1958, the Defense Advanced Research Projects Agency (DARPA) to make certain that the United States forever after maintained "a lead in applying state-of-the-art technology for military capabilities and to prevent technological surprise from her adversaries."[97]

Got it? People were scared of the Soviets, so they created a new satellite program run by a former Nazi. DARPA had also attracted attention from the *Los Angeles Times* in 2003 for some of its bad choices. As summarized in *Mother Jones*:

> In an August 2003 article, *Los Angeles Times* reporter Charles Pillar noted that DARPA[98] has put forth some of the "most boneheaded ideas ever to spring from the government"—including a "mechanical elephant" that never made it into the jungles of Vietnam and telepathy research that never quite afforded the U.S, the ability to engage in psychic spying.[99]

Although there have been spectacular failures, there have also been remarkable successes, such as the "M-16 rifle, Hellfire-missile-equipped Predator drones, stealth fighters and bombers, surface to surface artillery rocket systems, Tomahawk cruise missiles, B-52 bomber upgrades, Titan missiles, Javelin portable 'fire and forget' guided missiles and cannon-launched Copperhead guided projectiles,"[100] in addition to some of the most innovative consumer products, such as the internet, the global positioning system (GPS), stealth technology, and the computer mouse.[101]

DARPA has been called "the most creative place in our vast government for a scientist who wants to stretch his or her mind in adventurous directions and be well paid to do so."[102]

What did the brilliant minds at DARPA, those who'd failed to create a mechanical elephant but had created a computer mouse, think of Dr. Peter Daszak's idea to manipulate bat coronaviruses, then give the bats a vaccine made of "novel chimeric polyvalent recombinant spike proteins?"

Even the wild-eyed thinkers at DARPA thought the idea was crazy and dangerous and rejected the proposal.

*\*\*\**

In its rejection letter, DARPA noted many positive aspects of the project, such as the fact that Daszak's team had "plenty of prior experience," had "access to Yunan caves where bats are infected with SARSr viruses," had "carried out past surveillance work," and had "developed geo-based risk maps of zoonotic hotspots."[103]

In its rejection of the proposal, however, DARPA listed nine failings:

(1) The proposal is considered to potentially involve GoF/DURC [Gain of Function/ Dual Use Research of Concern] research because they propose to synthesize spike glycoproteins which bind to human cell receptors and insert them into SARSr-CoV backbones to assess whether they can cause SARS-like disease.

(2) However, the proposal does not mention or assess potential risks of Gain of Function (GoF) research.

(3) Nor does the proposal mention or assess Dual Use Research of Concern (DUCR) issues, and thus fails to present a DURC risk mitigation plan.

(4) The proposal hardly discusses ethical, legal, and social issues (ELSI).

(5) The proposal fails to discuss problems with the proposed vaccine delivery systems caused by the known issues of variability in vaccine dosage.

(6) The proposal did not provide sufficient information about how EHA [EcoHealth Alliance] would use any data obtained and how they would model development or perform any necessary statistical analysis.

(7) The proposal did not explain clearly how EHA will take advantage of their previous work, nor how that previous work could be extended.

(8) The proposal failed to clearly assess how it would deploy and validate the "TA2 preemption methods" in the wild. This refers to carrying out experiments with effective immune boosting molecules and delivery techniques via FEA [European Aerosol Federation] aerosolization mechanism at one test and

two control bat cave sites in Yunnan, China (PARC [Palo Alto Research Center Incorporated], EHA, WIV [Wuhan Institute of Virology]).

(9) The proposal does not address concerns about these vaccines not being able to protect against the wide variety of coronaviruses in bat caves which are constantly evolving, due to insufficient epitope coverage.[104]

In bureaucratic language, this rejection was nothing less than a smackdown of Dr. Peter Daszak's proposal. Daszak claimed this research did not involve gain of function research, but DARPA clearly disagreed. DARPA was further concerned by the lack of any plan to minimize risk and did not believe the vaccine strategy would work. It also seems that DARPA was highly skeptical of this airborne (aerosolized) vaccine, and even if all those concerns were alleviated, there was the question of how quickly these viruses evolved. The reviewers were also skeptical of the participation of the Wuhan Institute of Virology, as well as that of Dr. Shi Zheng Li, later to become known to the world in 2020 as the "bat lady of China" for her alleged role in creating SARS-CoV2 and causing the resulting COVID-19 epidemic. From the concluding remarks of the rejection letter:

> DRASTIC [a group of activists searching for the source of SARS-CoV-2] independently assesses that the tone of the proposal (see for instance the "our cave complex") and the deep suggested involvement of some of the WIV parties (Shi Zheng Li employed half-time for 3 years—paid via the grant—and invited to DARPA headquarters at Arlington), may not have helped either—especially in the absence of any DURC risk mitigation program.

It is clear that the proposed DEFUSE project led by Peter Daszak could have put local communities at risk by failing to consider the following issues:

- Gain of Function
- Dual Use Research of Concern
- Vaccine epitope coverage
- Regulatory requirements
- ELSI (ethical, legal, and social issues)
- Data usage[105]

One wonders if the world will be destroyed by evil or stupidity, and it seems to be a really close call. Daszak apparently considers the Yunnan caves harboring many bat coronaviruses to be something he jointly owns with the Chinese communist scientists. And Daszak seems to have had no problem letting his good friend Dr. Shi Zheng Li, the "bat lady of China," tag along with him to DARPA headquarters in Arlington, Virginia, as if it was "Take Your Daughter to Work Day." The only thing DARPA got wrong in its rejection was that Daszak's plan threatened not only local communities but the entire world.

But did this rejection from DARPA cause Daszak to abandon his plans?

No, it did not.

As reported in April 2020 by the *Daily Mail*, and now probably known to every person on Earth, it was revealed that the US National Institutes of Health had funded this research in Wuhan:

> The Wuhan Institute of Virology undertook corona-virus experiments on mammals captured more than 1,000 miles away in Yunnan which were funded by a $3.7 million grant from the U.S. government.
>
> Sequencing of the COVID-19 genome has traced it back to bats found in Yunnan caves, but it was first

thought to have transferred to humans at an animal market in Wuhan.

The revelation that the Wuhan Institute of Virology was experimenting on bats from the area already known to be the source of COVID-19—and doing so with American money—has sparked further fears that the lab, and not the market, is the original outbreak source.[106]

As of this writing, more than five million people have died from complications related to COVID-19. Should all those deaths be laid at the feet of Dr. Peter Daszak and those who allowed this research to go forward?

And where was our media, such as CNN, in getting to the bottom of these questions? They were actively supporting those who likely had caused this pandemic—and viciously attacking anyone who dared to ask questions.

\*\*\*

What was the role of Dr. Anthony Fauci throughout these events?

It has taken some time for facts to be revealed, but in late January 2022, Fox News, in a special report by Brett Baier, finally seemed to be interested in untangling this web of lies. The only rational conclusion that one can come to is that Anthony Fauci and his minions lied to America and the world throughout the pandemic. As a Fox reporter wrote:

According to the timeline of events laid out by Baier, Fauci was told on January 27, 2020 [about seven weeks before the nationwide lockdown] that his NIAID [National Institute of Allergy and Infectious Diseases] had been indirectly funding the Wuhan lab through

EcoHealth Alliance—a US-based scientific nonprofit that had been working with novel coronaviruses.

On January 31, Dr. Kristian Andersen, a noted virologist at Scripps Lab, privately told Fauci that after discussion with colleagues some of COVID-19's features look possibly engineered and the "genome is inconsistent with expectations from evolutionary theory."

Andersen added that the situation needed to be looked at more closely, at which point Fauci organized an all hands on deck conference call with colleagues where he was told that risky experiments with the novel coronavirus may not have gone through proper biosafety review and oversight.[107]

There are so many bombshells in this brief excerpt that it's difficult to know exactly where to begin. First, the United States was assisting this risky research, which had been proposed by an American scientist. Second, when looking at the genome, top scientists believed it was genetically manipulated. And third, this research had been likely been conducted without the proper oversight. The damning evidence against Fauci and other top leaders of America's public health system continued.

Hours later, Fauci hastily organized a call with dozens of worldwide virologists, and notes from the meeting obtained by *Special Report* reveal that suspicions of the lab leak theory were suppressed over concerns of how the public would react to news of possible Chinese involvement.

In the meeting, fears were raised by then-National Institutes of Health Director Francis Collins that "science and international harmony" could be harmed, and accusations of China's involvement could distract top researchers.

> Another scientist in the meeting dismissed the possibility that the virus jumped from a bat to a person in nature and pointed out that the virus could be generated in a lab much easier.[108]

Perhaps it's common in a crisis that people look to their leaders for reassurance. And yet, even when we do this, we must not allow our rational brain to be captured by the terror. The media is supposed to question the powerful, without fear or favor, to give us the truth. What is genuinely terrifying about these continuing revelations is apparently how little consideration was given to the question of the public's right to know.

Instead, the focus seemed to be on creating a narrative that is comforting to the ruling scientific elite: mother nature on a rampage, and brave scientists rushing to the scene of the disaster, like firemen running into a burning building trying to save as many lives as possible.

\*\*\*

Is there still more we do not fully understand about this story?

A January 20, 2022, article from the *National File* repeated claims that Dr. Peter Daszak and EcoHealth Alliance were actually a Central Intelligence Agency (CIA) front organization. The article detailed the claims of Dr. Andrew Huff, the former associate vice president of EcoHealth Alliance, made in a series of tweets he posted on January 12, 2022:

> For the record: In 2015 Dr. Peter Daszak stopped me as we were leaving work late at night and asked me if he should work with the CIA. I was shocked given my experience in security. Over the next 2 months he

gave me updates on 3 separate occasions about his work with the CIA.

When he asked me the question I stated "Peter, it never hurts to talk with them and there could potentially be money in it." Meanwhile, I was cringing that he told me this, in a non-classified setting (a SCIF [sensitive compartmented information facility]), to a person that was not "read-in," and to an uncleared person (me).

Then, over the next two months at the break area while getting coffee, or between meetings, he stated that they [CIA] were interested in the places that we were working, the people involved, the data that we were collecting, and that the work with them [CIA] was proceeding.[109]

These are shocking allegations. If true, they would go far in explaining why the US government (aside from President Trump) did not seem interested in pursuing the lab leak theory. Could there be some culpability, not just by Daszak and Fauci, but by the intelligence agencies as well? The allegations continued in the *National File* article:

Prior to the public statement earlier that morning, Huff took to twitter and claimed "members of the US government IC community have been harassing me, broke into my house, stole hard drives, and installed electronic surveillance devices throughout my house"...

In a separate series of posts, Huff said that he "wouldn't be surprised if the CIA/IC community organized the COVID coverup acting as an intermediary between Fauci, Collins, Daszak, [Dr. Ralph] Baric [of the University of North Carolina], and many others. At best, it was the biggest criminal conspiracy in US history by bureaucrats or political appointees."[110]

In chapter six we will address the question of which role the intelligence agencies might have played in the coverage of COVID and other highly charged political issues.

*\*\**

CNN was without a doubt the tip of the spear in attacking those who asked questions about Fauci's narrative on COVID-19. The network did so through simultaneously stoking fear with its death chart and belittling those who asked reasonable questions. Aside from a few reporters and commentators, the mainstream media largely bought the story cooked up by Fauci and his crew that COVID-19 likely had a natural origin, even though the bats that carried the precursor virus lived more than a thousand miles from Wuhan.

Why did the media go along with this obvious falsehood so willingly?

In 2016, STAT, a health and medicine oriented website, reported that drug and vaccine makers spent more than $5 billion a year in advertising. STAT reported:

> The data paint a revealing picture of a booming industry. Drug advertisers worship at the altar of TV. They're relentless in hawking their top products to the aging baby boomers watching network shows. But they're also spending more to reach niche audiences. It's not unusual for drug makers to make six figure buys in magazines like Family Handyman or the celebrity tabloid Star, or on cable TV channels such as Country Music Television or the Hallmark Channel.[111]

Regardless of what you like to watch, the drug makers will figure out how to advertise to you. In 2016, broadcast networks ABC, NBC, CBS, and Fox reported $740 million in advertising revenue from Big Pharma, and the cable networks received $380 million—for a total of $1.12 billion.[112] Although we do not have the figures broken down by television network for 2020, Kanter Media reported that total Big Pharma TV advertising for that year was a whopping $4.58 billion.[113]

Where does all of this leave the public?

We have our leading figures in public health, like Anthony Fauci and Francis Collins, covering up reasonable investigations for fear of offending the Chinese or lowering the public's opinion of scientists.

Then we have news outlets that get massive amounts of ad revenue from Big Pharma, and because of this it seems there's a great reluctance to question any assertions about public health. It's a much better financial decision for the networks to stoke fear and division, then sell the product that will supposedly save us, like the COVID-19 vaccines. Leave the hard questions to the conspiracy theorists.

The simple reality the public needs to acknowledge is that few in the media or government are genuinely looking out for our well-being.

They do not *want* to inform us.

They want to scare us and make us submissive.

It would seem that media and the government have learned that fearmongering makes us so much easier to control.

# CHAPTER FIVE

# CNN's White House Connections and Digital Intelligence Group

What is the proper relationship between any White House administration and the various news organizations?

While some may think of this as a superficial question, one of personalities rather than politics, there is much more to it. We often feel that we become as familiar with politicians and journalists as with members of our own family, often with similar levels of trust from our end. However, we should not simply assume those in power, whether in government or the press, are acting responsibly. We think this problem should be easy to navigate, and yet it seems that the failure to understand these dangerous relationships is dangerous to democracy.

We need our media and journalists to hold the powerful to account. It is simply to be expected that when one political group gains enormous power it will inevitably try to corrupt the press into giving it favorable coverage. Why should we expect human beings to act against their interests? That is why any attempt at censorship or any collusion of power centers with the media strikes at the very bedrock of our civic life.

One of the earliest American examples of the importance of being able to think and speak freely came in a letter that Benjamin Franklin had printed in 1722 under the pseudonym Silence Dogood. Franklin had written the letter in response to the jailing of his brother, who had criticized the Massachusetts government for its failure to capture a pirate ship that was raiding the colonies. Franklin wrote:

> Without Freedom of Thought, there can be no such Thing as Wisdom; and no such Thing as publick Liberty. Without Freedom of Speech, which is the Right of every Man, as far as by it, he does not hurt or controul the Right of another: And this is the only Check it ought to suffer, and the only Bounds it ought to know.

> This sacred Privilege is so essential to free Govern-ments, that the Security of Property, and the Freedom of Speech always go together. And in those wretched Countries where a Man cannot call his Tongue his own, he can scarce call any Thing else his own. Whoever would overthrow the Liberty of a Nation, must begin by subduing the Freeness of Speech, a *Thing* terrible to Publick Traytors.[114]

Franklin can be rightfully credited as one of the first American thinkers to explicitly link freedom of thought and speech to the greater health of society. While tyrants and despots cry out that there needs to be a single authoritative voice, and that if speakers do not conform to their edicts they should not be given any platform, whether in the digital world or the various state and national capitols. Franklin is adamant that the freedom to think and speak according to the dictates of one's conscience precedes *all* other freedoms.

It is by understanding this founding principle that we understand why the First Amendment to the Constitution enshrined the right of the citizens to think and speak without fear of government reprisal:

> Congress shall make no law respecting an establishment of religion, or prohibiting the free exercise thereof; or abridging the freedom of speech, or of the press; or the right of the people to peaceably assemble, and to petition the government for a redress of grievances.[115]

The First Amendment is truly remarkable in the long history of nations. Instead of religious wars, the framers left the decision of what constituted genuine faith up to God. We are not infallible creatures who can be expected to render a decision on a person's religious beliefs. The First Amendment made it clear that Americans were free to think and speak as they wished and that those opinions could be expressed in the press. In addition, Americans have the right to peacefully assemble and call on their leaders to listen to their complaints.

That is how you put together a stable society. Removing these rights is how you begin to control a society.

How strong is the right of the press to report on government misconduct? This question was put to the test in 1971 during the "Pentagon Papers" case. The US Department of Defense commissioned a study to examine American involvement in Vietnam from 1945 to 1967. The study was completed in early 1969, and in 1971 the *New York Times* and the *Washington Post* had obtained copies of this report and were looking to publish excerpts. The Nixon administration sought to block publication and appealed to the US Supreme Court.

In a six-to-three decision, the Supreme Court upheld the right of these newspapers to publish the report. Justice Hugo Black wrote of the principle involved:

In the First Amendment, the Founding Fathers gave the free press the protection it must have to fulfill its essential role in our democracy. The press was to serve the governed, not the governors. The government's power to censor the press was abolished so that the press would remain forever free to censure the government. The press was protected so that it could bare the secrets of government and inform the people. Only a free and unrestrained press can effectively expose deception in government. And paramount among the responsibilities of a free press is the duty to prevent any part of the government from deceiving the people and sending them off to distant lands to die of foreign fevers and foreign shot and shell.[116]

While the Pentagon Papers case reassures us that the media can confront the powerful, the question remains if this is the only possible danger in the press-government relationship. Normally, when we think of the clash, it's the media trying to publish something the government does not want revealed, and the government responding with force.

However, there is another danger. What if the media, in the course of reporting, become too close to the government? How would the American public know that their watchdog over the government had, in effect, become its lapdog? How would the public know if the loyalty of the media had switched from defending the people to protecting the powerful?

This book clearly demonstrates the bias that CNN had against the Trump administration. But that administration is now gone and a new one is in place. What kind of a relationship does CNN have with the Biden administration?

Cary and Kent have conducted an in-depth investigation of this question, and their findings are troubling, but also indicative of a pattern abundantly documented in this book.

It's not simply that the members of the Biden administration prefer CNN over Fox News, but that they prefer CNN over all other news outlets.

\*\*\*

Cary's and Kent's investigation revealed that several members of Biden's cabinet and White House are actively following employees at all levels of CNN on social media; not just news anchors but also producers and editors.

This pattern is *not* being replicated with Fox, NBC, CBS, the *New York Times*, the *Washington Post*, or Al Jazeera. These outlets are generally being followed on Twitter and Instagram, but there seem to be no other examples of Biden Cabinet or White House staff directly following specific journalists, production staff, or senior executives of news agencies.

Cary and Kent observed forty-seven Biden administration Twitter accounts, analyzing more than 30,000 accounts, and discovered seven Biden administration members who were following CNN-associated individuals directly, not on their news-outlet Twitter accounts. Therefore, the authors consider these to be direct associations between individuals.

Marcia Fudge is the secretary of Housing and Urban Development for the Biden administration and is directly following Tori Blase, a CNN supervisor and executive producer. Blase has been with CNN for twenty-eight years, and it is unclear why Fudge would be directly following her.

Jennifer Granholm, the secretary of Energy, is directly following news anchors Jake Tapper, Don Lemon, and Victor Blackwell on their Twitter accounts.

Jen Psaki, the former White House press secretary, was directly following Jake Tapper.

Michael Regan, the administrator of the Environmental Protection Agency (EPA), is following Laura Jarrett, a CNN anchor based in Washington, DC.

Ron Klain, the White House chief of staff, is a long-time Facebook friend of CNN anchor Dana Bash.

Probably most concerning is Symone Sanders, the former spokesperson for Vice President Kamala Harris. On Twitter she was following Patrick Oppmann, CNN's Havana-based correspondent and CNN's Havana bureau chief. She is also following Chip Grabow, a senior editor for CNN whose job duties include editing and approving scripts for broadcast and digital content. On Instagram, she's following CNN planning producer Janelle Griffin-Butts, CNN photojournalist Jay McMichael, CNN anchor for international news Zain Asher, CNN correspondent Josh Campbell, CNN chief international correspondent Clarissa Ward, CNN national correspondent Rene March, anchor of CNN's *Early Start* Laura Jarret, CNN anchors Jake Tapper and Don Lemon, and CNN anchor and correspondent Amara Walker.

Does CNN have a "special relationship" with the Biden White House, one not even enjoyed by its natural ideological allies, such as the *New York Times* or the *Washington Post*?

\*\*\*

Who is Symone Sanders and why might she be so important to understanding the friendly connections between CNN and the Biden White House?

During the 2016 presidential campaign, she was the national press secretary for Democratic presidential candidate Senator Bernie Sanders. She left the campaign in late June 2016, making a statement shortly afterwards that "she was not let go and that leaving the campaign was her decision."

Four months later, in October 2016 she was hired as a Democratic strategist and political commentator at CNN, a position she would hold until April 2019 when she joined the Biden campaign for president as a senior advisor. After Biden won the election in November 2020, there was speculation Sanders might be appointed White House press secretary, which would make her the first African American woman in that position. However, that position was filled by Jen Psaki, a decision that Bakari Sellers, a friend of Sanders, claimed "stung" Sanders and that she was "hurt" about being passed over.

In 2019, *Politico* ran a long piece on Sanders titled "Why Symone Sanders Went from Bernie to Biden," establishing her as a rising superstar among political operatives:

> In one sense, the 30-year-old Symone Sanders is very much a recognizable Washington character, the archetype of an ambitious young operative: comfortable in front of a camera, unafraid to claim a slot as the voice of a grassroots activist community and very conscious of her brand.
>
> In another, though, she's an object of curiosity. In 2016 she hit the national stage as press secretary for Bernie Sanders, the uncompromising outsider whose progressive crusade galvanized the American left. This year, she's a senior advisor and cable TV surrogate for Joe Biden, the centrist candidate whom Bernie supporters widely see as a rebuke, even a threat, to their entire mission.[117]

The question to ask of Symone Sanders is whether she is practical or amoral. Does she have any unshakeable values, or is she willing to go wherever she can amass the most power? Or is there a third option, a mixing of the two, expressing the view once espoused by conservative godfather William F. Buckley that he would support the most conservative candidate who had a chance of winning?

Instead of being appointed White House press secretary, Sanders was given the position of "Senior Advisor and Chief Spokesperson to

Vice President Kamala Harris." Sanders did not last long in this position, announcing on December 2, 2021, her intention to leave before the end of the month. Her departure from the Harris office was the second high-profile resignation, coming shortly after the announced resignation of Ashley Etienne, the vice president's communications director.

Perhaps the one-sided pattern of media contacts on the part of the Biden administration can be explained by its myopic view of only trying to appeal to one side of the aisle and avoiding the tough questions that might be posed by political opponents.

The Biden administration claims to reach out to all Americans; yet this pattern of focusing near exclusively on CNN through administration members' social networks suggests that there are favored and disfavored friends in the Fourth Estate.

One does not unify a country by speaking to only half the population.

\*\*\*

Is CNN planning to develop its own cyber capabilities to wage a digital war against its media enemies or those in public life with whom it disagrees?

Will CNN soon start employing robots, rather than journalists, to write its stories?

Let's begin first with the way CNN describes the operations of its digital intelligence group. This article is written by Kelly Davis, an engineer with CNN's digital intelligence unit. We must assume it is published with the approval of her employer. She begins:

> At CNN, our mission is to inform, engage, and empower the world in a way that is trusted, timely, and transparent. This mission is more critical than ever as we face some of the most challenging times of our generation. As the world is increasingly digital

in nature, we are relentlessly focusing our mission to directly connect with our audience, understand what they care about most, and reach them in a way that is most accessible for their lifestyle. Our Data Intelligence Team, in particular, leverages data and machine-learning capabilities to build innovative experiences for our audience and provides scalable solutions to CNN's operations.[118]

You might read the above passage at face value and believe that CNN is simply trying to better serve its audience. Or you can see the possibility of using machine learning (another term for artificial intelligence) as a way to continue its pattern of deception. For those unfamiliar with machine learning, it's based on the idea that systems can learn from data, identify patterns, and make decisions with minimal human intervention. The goal is that when these systems are exposed to new data they can adapt independently. This is also what people fear the most. Let's take a little deeper look into CNN's explanation of what it was doing:

Initially, our process for training a new experimental model was fairly similar to our process for (re) training a production model. This process was optimized for consistently training production models at scale, and did really well at that. Unfortunately, it was not designed for lightweight experimentation, and because of that, the research iteration process was frustratingly slow.

Partnering with the folks at Hop Labs we explored a number of platforms and approaches to streamlining this.[119]

The next important question is: What is "Hop Labs" and what does it do? The Hop Labs website describes its work in detail. In the "Work

We've Done" section, it lists CNN as one of its clients, as well as the United Nations. This ties the CNN Digital Intelligence Unit directly to the United Nations. This is how Hop Labs describes its work:

> We've successfully deployed production-grade machine-learning systems in the fashion, retail, and healthcare industries. We've also deployed advanced analytics systems that are actively used worldwide. And our product studio team has helped a number of innovative startups and organizations bring their first product or digital experience to market.
>
> As meaningful as it is to be deeply involved in adding to the core of a client's business, it also means that we can't always speak publicly to the work we've done. We're often solving problems our client's customers and competitors don't yet know they have, and the approach we use is usually proprietary.[120]

It would appear that CNN is using Hop Labs not only to identify trends, but also exploring how to generate news articles based on algorithmically generated data. In other words, one day your news might be written by a computer, who sucked up a bunch of information, used its artificial intelligence to write like a person, then fed it to you, hoping you would believe it was written by a human being.

Does this sound like science fiction? It's not. In fact, it's already here, as detailed in a *Forbes* magazine article from 2019. After artificial intelligence (AI) was first deployed in business reporting by *Bloomberg News* and *Forbes*, it expanded to other outlets.

> The Washington Post also has a robot reporting system called Heliograf. In its first year, it produced approximately 850 articles and earned The Post an award for its "Excellence in Use of Bots" from its work on the 2016 election coverage. However, the Post is

using their system to not replace journalists, but to assist them and make their jobs easier and faster. The Heliograf can detect trends in finance and big data to alert reporters to give them a heads-up for reporting. Like how The LA Times is using AI to report on earthquakes based on data from the U.S. geological survey and also tracks homicide information on every homicide committed in the city of Los Angeles.[121]

Artificial intelligence can not only detect trends in data and write articles, it can also be a detective.

On February 19, 2022, the *New York Times* reported how machine learning and artificial intelligence were used to identify the mysterious Q, inspiration for the QAnon phenomenon, which preceded the 2020 presidential election. One of the people suspected of starting QAnon was a man named Paul Furber; he may have been inspired by a message on an online message board that read, "Many in our government worship Satan."[122]

The outlandish claim made perfect sense to Mr. Furber, a South African software developer and tech journalist long fascinated with American politics and conspiracy theories, he said in an interview. He still clung to "Pizzagate," the debunked online lie that liberal Satanists were trafficking children from a Washington restaurant. He was also among the few who understood an obscure reference in the message to "Operation Mockingbird," an alleged C.I.A. scheme to manipulate the news media.[123]

The *New York Times* article is a genuinely good exploration of the field of whether a writer can be identified simply by comparing his or her writing to other known examples by that writer. Machine learning was even used to reveal that J. K. Rowling, the creator of the Harry

Potter series of children's books, had written a 2013 mystery, *Cuckoo's Calling*, under another name.[124]

The first reporter to break a story is usually the one who gets all the glory. Can we expect media organizations not to use this new technology to try and scoop the competition?

As far as the researchers for this book have been able to determine, CNN employs at least 220 employees on its Digital Intelligence Unit. The senior and executive staff at CNN on the Digital Intelligence Unit are vice president for Machine Learning and Data Platform Deepna Devkar,[125] senior manager for Audience Intelligence/Digital Research Krystal Paden,[126] director of Machine Learning Bo Williams,[127] senior machine learning data scientist Miguel Perez,[128] senior director for Machine Learning and AI Ashok Chandrashekar,[129] and tech lead for machine learning operations Kelly Davis.[130]

The senior and executive staff at WarnerMedia (parent company of CNN) for the Digital Intelligence group are senior vice president for Data Science and Machine Learning Engineering Haile Owusu[131] and director for Risk Assessments and Testing Edwin Covert.[132]

Of the people listed, it is Edwin Covert who raises the most questions about the use of cybersecurity specialists at CNN and its parent company. His LinkedIn profile identifies him as working for the US Navy from August 1992 to August 1996 as a "Cryptologic Technician Interpretive," an intelligence-related position. From September 2011 to June 2016, he worked for Booz Allen Hamilton (the same contractor who employed Edward Snowden) as a senior lead technologist, a cyber- and intelligence-related position. He has also worked for Warner Bros. and Deutsche Bank in the cybersecurity realm. However, the researchers for this book have come across information that leads them to believe that Covert has also been an operator for Tailored Access Operations (TAO), now Computer Network Operations, structured as an "S32," which is a cyber-warfare intelligence-gathering unit of the National Security Agency (NSA). According to a 2013 article in *Foreign Policy*, TAO had become "increasingly accomplished at its mission, thanks in part to the high-level cooperation it receives from the 'big three' American telecom companies (AT&T, Verizon, and Sprint), most of the large US-based internet service providers, and many of the top computer security software manufacturers and consulting companies."

Our researchers also believe that Covert was a Counterintelligence Special Agent Course instructor in 2004, as well as employed by the US Army Electronic Warfare Test Directorate as a Department of Defense civilian. There are also two other troubling connections of people tied into cybersecurity, whose skill sets suggest that the true intention is not cyber-defense, but cyber-warfare.

The first is Jeff Yang, who currently works for CNN as a "columnist and opinion writer." His regular job is with the Rand Corporation's Institute for the Future (IFTF), where he is in charge of the digital intelligence team. This is from the IFTF website:

> IFTF Research Director Jeff Yang heads up our Digital Intelligence Team. As a leading strategist in communications and consumer insights, digital media, and emerging technologies, Jeff has spent much of his career leading the development and application of integrated qualitative and quantitative tools to identify future cultural impact around social connections and consumer trends.... Jeff holds a bachelor's degree in Psychology from Harvard University and was a Harvard National Scholar with coursework in Asian languages, literature, and civilizations, media studies, and economics.[133]

The Rand Corporation is a well-known defense contractor (it was hired by the Pentagon in 1967 to review what had gone wrong in the Vietnam War, thus generating the Pentagon Papers, which were ultimately leaked to the media by Daniel Ellsberg) and maintains an entire division of intelligence professionals tasked with conducting war games.[134]

War games are analytic games that simulate aspects of warfare at the tactical, operational, or strategic level. It is likely that CNN is using warfighting concepts to train, educate, and analyze scenarios, as well as assess how force planning and posture choices affect campaign outcomes.

If this is accurate, the question becomes: Why is a news organization engaging in war games when its mission should be to seek the truth?

The second person of concern is Diede de Kok, a senior intelligence specialist at WarnerMedia. This is how she describes herself on LinkedIn:

> I am a problem solver that loves to be challenged. My expertise is diverse; I have experience working on Safety and Security Management, preventing extremist recruitment and gang violence, working with Human Rights and transitional justice, and non-violent resistance.[135]

Her LinkedIn profile details her work at Pax Ludens from May 2014 to March 2015 as having "managed the Mainstream Mapping during the simulation games, debriefed the participants during the simulation games," and "improved the method of Mainstream Mapping and debriefing."[136]

In the simplest terms, this means she was deeply involved in the war games that Pax Ludens was running.

In addition, it should be noted that Pax Ludens is a well-known military-industrial complex, third-party intelligence subcontractor.

The undeniable fact is that CNN has a digital intelligence group of at least 220 individuals, and that Cary, Kent, and their researchers have been able to identify at least three of them with likely intelligence agency involvement in wargaming strategy and deception.

This raises the question of why these people would be working for a news agency.

Chapter Six delves more deeply into the question of how much influence or control the intelligence agencies may have over CNN.

# CNN Hires Intelligence Spooks. Or Is It the Reverse?

Many of today's CNN viewers know Carl Bernstein as the older political analyst who often appeared on various shows during the Trump administration to promote the Russia collusion narrative as "worse than Watergate"[137] or declare that Trump is a "war criminal."[138] Carl Bernstein is a legendary figure in journalism, being half of the investigative team at the *Washington Post*, with Bob Woodward, who broke the story of the Watergate scandal, which eventually resulted in the resignation of President Richard Nixon on August 8, 1974.

However, in the Trump era, Bernstein became something of a joke, claiming that the Russia collusion story, President Trump's call with Ukrainian President Volodymyr Zelensky, Trump's response to the COVID-19 crisis, and Trump's phone call with the Georgia secretary of state in the wake of the disputed 2020 election were all "worse than Watergate" or had "echoes of Watergate."[139]

None of this is to take away from the remarkable body of work Bernstein has created over his decades in journalism. Aside from his work on Watergate, probably the most important story he wrote was a 25,000-word piece in *Rolling Stone* magazine on October 20, 1977, which examined how the CIA worked with the American media. In 2022, it's ironic how conservatives are the ones who distrust the intelligence services, while in the 1960s and 1970s, it was the liberals who distrusted not only the intelligence agencies but also the influence of large corporations.

Bernstein's *Rolling Stone* article opened with what was a bombshell when it was released:

> In 1953, Joseph Alsop, then one of America's leading syndicated columnists, went to the Philippines to cover an election. He did not go because he was asked to do so by his syndicate. He did not go because he was asked to do so by the newspapers that printed his column. He went at the request of the CIA.[140]

To the American public of 1977 this was a shocking accusation. If there is a wall between church and state, there is supposed to be an equally high wall between the media and the government, particularly the intelligence services like the CIA, which are not supposed to be operating in the United States.

It's difficult to think of anything less democratic than an intelligence agency guiding news coverage.

One begins to suspect that the common claim by America's adversaries during the Cold War, that many US journalists were in fact spies, has some degree of validity.

Bernstein further detailed how extensive the CIA's influence operation was, as well as the level at which the media of the time cooperated:

> Alsop is one of more than 400 American journalists who in the past twenty-five years have secretly carried out assignments for the Central Intelligence Agency, according to documents on file at CIA headquarters.

Some of these journalists' relationships with the Agency were tacit; some were explicit. There was cooperation, accommodation and overlap. Journalists provided a full range of clandestine services—from simple intelligence gathering to serve as go-betweens with spies in Communist countries. Reporters shared their notebooks with the CIA. Editors shared their staff. Some of the journalists were Pulitzer Prize winners.[141]

Some might say that all this proves is that during the Cold War, American journalists were patriotic. And yet, truth, not patriotism, is supposed to be the proper field of interest for the news industry. Members of the news media are not supposed to parrot narratives simply because they are helpful to the government. They're supposed to give the public the facts. Bernstein continued with his account of this CIA-media alliance:

Most were less exalted: foreign correspondents who found that their association with the Agency helped their work; stringers and freelancers who were as interested in the derring-do of the spy business as in filing articles; and, in the smallest category, full-time CIA employees masquerading as journalists abroad. In many instances, CIA documents show, journalists were engaged to perform tasks with the consent of the management of America's leading news organizations.[142]

Again, while it is important to note that these actions took place in the shadow of the Cold War, they establish a pattern of US intelligence agencies being willing to co-opt American media in order to further their objectives. There is ample evidence in recent American history that certain lines will be crossed, by both the intelligence services and the media, such as the lies told about progress in Vietnam, the presence of weapons of mass destruction in Iraq, or whether we were "turning the corner" during our twenty year war in Afghanistan.

Although Bernstein's article was extensive, he was frustrated by the fact that there was much information he could not obtain about the true scope of this work by the CIA, as the CIA claimed that to reveal this information would be embarrassing to those who helped it. However, Bernstein was able to confirm the names of many top executives, including "William Paley of the Columbia Broadcasting System [CBS], Henry Luce of Time, Inc., Arthur Hays Sulzberger of the *New York Times*, Barry Bingham Sr. of the *Louisville-Courier Journal*, and James Copley of the Copley News Services."[143] These were some of the largest names in news of their day, and suggests that the media were often willing participants in their work with the CIA. Bernstein continued with his list:

> Other organizations which cooperated with the CIA include the American Broadcasting Company [ABC], the National Broadcasting Company [NBC], the Associated Press, United Press International, Reuters, Hearst Newspapers, Scripps-Howard, the *Miami Herald* and the old *Saturday Evening Post* and *New York Herald-Tribune*.
>
> By far the most valuable of these associations, according to CIA officials, have been with the *New York Times*, CBS, and Time Inc.
>
> The CIA's use of the American news media has been much more extensive than Agency officials have acknowledged publicly or in closed sessions with members of Congress.[144]

When reading the list of the media outlets that cooperated with the CIA, it makes one wonder if there were any that did not. This alliance seems to be part of the game, but the public was not made aware of these rules, even when our elected officials conducted their own investigations. As Bernstein wrote:

> During the 1976 investigation of the CIA by the Senate Intelligence Committee, chaired by Senator Frank Church, the dimensions of the Agency's Involvement became apparent to several members of the panel, as well as two or three investigators on the staff. But top officials of the CIA, including former directors William Colby and George Bush [Reagan's two-term vice president, and US president from 1989 to 1993], persuaded the committee to restrict its inquiry into the matter and to deliberately misrepresent the scope of the activities in its final report.[145]

George Bush, who lied to the Church Committee about the scope of CIA involvement with the American media during the Cold War, somehow made his way onto the Reagan ticket as vice president, and then became president in his own right.

Aside from being in favor of the CIA's anti-communist crusade, the question that remains is why it seemed that the relationship between the CIA and the media functioned so smoothly. The spooks seemed to love the media, and the journalists loved the spooks. Bernstein suggests it's due to their common worldview and added this:

> Within the CIA, journalist-operatives were accorded elite status, a consequence of the common experience journalists shared with high-level CIA officials. Many had gone to the same schools as their CIA handlers, moved in the same circles, shared fashionably liberal, anticommunist political values, and were part of the same "old boy" network that constituted something of

KENT HECKENLIVELY AND CARY POARCH

an establishment in the media, politics and academia of postwar America.[146]

This piece from 1977 sounds right at home in much of the political dialogue of 2022, except that it would likely be coming from the mouth of a conservative Republican (or somebody designated as "alt-right" or a "conspiracy theorist") rather than a journalist with impeccable liberal credentials.

How is it that the Left has so completely forgotten its historic concerns about the lies of the intelligence community, and how is it that the Right has so embraced this position?

\*\*\*

A quote widely attributed to Ronald Reagan's CIA director, William Casey, from February 1981 is, "We'll know our disinformation program is complete when everything the American public believes is false."[147]

While it is difficult to pin down the accuracy of this quote (it seems strong to us), there is little doubt that one of the leading columnists of his day, Jack Anderson, had a deep and abiding suspicion not only of William Casey, but of the CIA in general. On September 22, 1981, Anderson had a column titled "CIA's Misleading Tactics," in which he wrote:

> In a triple assault on the public's right to know, the Central Intelligence Agency is (1) trying to shut off channels of information to the electorate, (2) seeking criminal penalties against reporters whose stories might identify CIA operatives and (3) spreading "disinformation" to news agencies.

> The most disturbing is the disinformation campaign. This poisons the well from which Americans draw the facts they need to govern themselves. The wise Thomas

Jefferson sought to lay this issue to rest two centuries ago when he argued that the people's right to know is more important than the officials' right to govern.

Now along comes Bill Casey, the doddering CIA director, with the argument that the government has the right to mislead the public by planting phony stories in the press.[148]

William Casey had a habit of mumbling when he talked, which is why so many of his pronouncements were subject to great debate. Casey was Reagan's campaign manager during the 1980 election and served as head of the CIA until December 15, 1986, when he suffered two seizures and was later diagnosed with a brain tumor. He had been scheduled to testify before Congress the day after his two seizures struck him down, on the burgeoning Iran-Contra crisis. Casey died of his brain tumor on May 6, 1987, never testifying about what he knew of the two parts of the Iran-Contra affair: first, the sale of weapons to so-called moderates in Iran in return for their help in freeing some American hostages held in Lebanon, and second, the diversion of money from those sales to anticommunist rebels in Nicaragua.

Carl Bernstein's former partner, Bob Woodward, became very interested in the CIA under William Casey and wrote a bestselling book, *Veil: The Secret Wars of the CIA, 1981–1987*, which was the result of many conversations with the elderly spy chief.

Near the end of his more than five-hundred-page book, Woodward summed up his opinions of the aged spy chief, who'd actually worked as an agent for the precursor to the CIA, the Office of Strategic Services (OSS) in World War II:

The previous year Casey told me he had read a review I had written of John le Carré's *A Perfect Spy*. Casey said he agreed with my interpretation of the le Carré view of espionage, that the better the spying, the better the

> deception. I had quoted him one of my favorite lines
> in the book, "In every operation there is an above the
> line and a below the line. Above the line is what you
> do by the book. Below the line is how you do the job."
> Casey just took it in, an intense, almost gloomy, look
> on his face. He could be so distant. What did he think?
> I had asked. No response. Did he agree? Nothing.[149]

The principle that intelligence agencies have procedures to follow and that they often abandon them to accomplish worthwhile goals is both a strength and a weakness. This need is understandable in the hypothetical realm, but what happens when this godlike power is exercised by actual flesh-and-blood human beings? It's understood that this is done, but even the spy chief doesn't want to attempt an answer to such a question.

Do we act, or do we wait to see what develops? Each has its risks.

Still, as described by Woodward, Casey had some admirable traits as a spy chief in a democracy.

> Casey had been an attractive figure to me because he
> was useful and because he never avoided a confron-
> tation. He might shout and challenge, even threaten,
> but he never broke off the dialogue or the relationship.
> Back in 1985 when we had exposed the covert preemp-
> tive teams to strike against terrorists he had said to me,
> "You'll probably have blood on your hands before it's
> over." That was, I later learned, after Casey had worked
> secretly with the Saudi intelligence service and its
> ambassador in Washington to arrange the assassination
> of the arch-terrorist Fadlallah. Instead of Fadlallah, the
> car bomb had killed at least eighty people.[150]

It's an awesome power to be in control of an intelligence agency—and yet still have to engage with the members of the press, who seek to question your actions and reveal your secrets. This is the tension that unfortunately exists in every democracy today, and it seems as if Casey handled it as well as any person might be expected to do. However, if one chooses to use such power, he must also accept the consequences.

Woodward seems to believe that Casey exceeded the scope of his power, not simply by disregarding procedures but by breaking an understanding, if not the law, about the actions expected of the CIA. The public expects the intelligence agencies to provide the president with information to make decisions. But the public does not expect them to collaborate with other intelligence agencies in the secret killing of potential enemies. Woodward writes:

> How did he [Casey] square that? I imagined, and hoped, he felt the moral dilemma. How could he not? He was too smart not to see that he and the White House had broken the rules, if not the law. It was Casey who had blood on his hands.[151]

In the end, Woodward could provide no definitive answer about whether Casey, or the CIA itself, felt the full weight of the moral dilemmas they had created by their actions.

Who is the villain and who is the hero of this tale? Is the villain the intelligence agencies, and the press the hero? Or vice versa? The public may not ever know the answer to that question. However, in light of the mistakes that the intelligence agencies have made over the years, Americans must continue the conversation, even if at times we shout at each other.

\*\*\*

Determining what's really going on with the intelligence agencies can be difficult because transparency really isn't their thing. Avoiding transparency is built into the very fabric of being an intelligence agency.

KENT HECKENLIVELY AND CARY POARCH

Therefore, this section is conservative in its conclusions. However, Cary and Kent are not shy about sharing their suspicions. It's an axiom of human nature that when you allow people and organizations to work in the dark, some of them will do very bad things. There is no reason to believe the members of the intelligence community are immune to this common human failing.

On March 14, 2016, President Barack Obama signed Executive Order 13721, "Developing an Integrated Global Engagement Center to Support Government-Wide Counterterrorism Communications Activities Directed Abroad and Revoking Executive Order 13584."[152] The measure was claimed to be necessary to combat the information activities of the Islamic State of Iraq and the Levant (ISIL), Al-Qaida, and other violent Islamic groups. Many worried that this Global Engagement Center might just as easily be turned against American citizens as against Islamic terrorists.

However, when reading the text of Obama's executive order, it seems the government was being exceedingly careful in trying to balance these competing interests:

> Recognizing the need for innovation and new approaches to counter the messaging and diminish the influence of ISIL, Al-Qa'ida, and other violent extremists abroad, and in order to protect the vital national interests of the United States, while also recognizing the importance of protections for freedom of expression, including those under the First Amendment to the Constitution of the United States and international human rights obligation....[153]

So, where's the problem? Most agree about the need to fight terrorism, as well as protecting freedom of speech, and both are acknowledged in Obama's executive order.

However, the government website for the Global Engagement Center sends a significantly different message. This is how the center describes its core mission:

> To direct, lead, synchronize, integrate, and coordinate efforts of the Federal Government to recognize, understand, expose, and counter foreign state and non-state propaganda and disinformation efforts aimed at undermining or influencing the policies, security, or stability of the United States, its allies, and partner nations.[154]

Can you detect the difference in language between Obama's executive order and the current website for the Global Engagement Center, housed at the US Department of State? The executive order talked about diminishing "the influence of ISIL, Al-Qa'ida, and other violent extremists abroad" while the current website talks about the effort to "counter foreign state and non-state propaganda and disinformation efforts aimed at undermining or influencing the policies, security, or stability of the United States...."

What happened to the need to fight "violent extremists?"

With a little fancy lawyering, it would be easy to justify propaganda against many legitimate political groups in the United States.

How did the rules change?

No need to guess. The government told us in late December 2016. You might have missed it because it happened right around Christmas, just after Donald Trump beat Hillary Clinton in the presidential election, and the country had safely passed through the effort by Democrats to use "faithless electors" to swing the Electoral College vote to Clinton.

But Obama's allies in the US Senate, Republican Rob Portman from Ohio and Democrat Chris Murphy from Connecticut, were only too happy to announce the change in the mission of the Global

Engagement Center in a December 23, 2016, press release on Senator Portman's official website:

> U.S. Senators Rob Portman (R-OH) and Chris Murphy (D-CT) today announced that their Countering Disinformation and Propaganda Act—legislation designed to help American allies counter foreign government propaganda from Russia, China, and other nations—has been signed into law as part of the FY 2017 National Defense Authorization Act (NDAA) Conference Report.
>
> The bipartisan bill, which was introduced by Senators Portman and Murphy in March, will improve the ability of the United States to counter foreign propaganda and disinformation from our enemies by establishing an interagency center housed at the State Department to coordinate and synchronize counter-propaganda throughout the U.S. government. To support these efforts, the bill also creates a grant program for NGOs, think tanks, civil society and other experts outside government who are engaged in counter-propaganda related work.[155]

With the changed requirements from fighting violent Muslim groups to any disinformation that might conceivably be tied to Russia or China, a new strategy could be deployed. The players could be any people "outside government who are engaged in counter-propaganda related work."

It wouldn't be a stretch to argue that the intelligence community had put together an "insurance policy" just ahead of the incoming Trump administration.

\*\*\*

The January 3, 2017, episode of *The Rachel Maddow Show* on MSNBC had the following remarkable exchange between Maddow and Democratic Senator Chuck Schumer from New York about the incoming Trump administration.

> SENATOR CHUCK SCHUMER: So, I am, I was distraught after the election. But now I'm actually invigorated by the challenge and our ability to succeed in this challenge.

> RACHEL MADDOW: Let me ask you. I don't know if you've seen this. I don't want to blindside you with this. This is the latest statement, latest tweet as you were just saying—President-Elect's latest unsolicited pronouncement on the intelligence community. This was his tweet just a little while ago tonight. You can see the scare quotes there. *"The 'Intelligence' briefings on so called 'Russian hacking' was delayed until Friday. Perhaps more time needed to build a case. Very strange."* (Emphasis added.)

> We're actually told—intelligence sources tell NBC News that since this tweet has been posted, that actually, this intelligence briefing for the President-Elect was always planned for Friday. It hasn't been delayed. But he's taking these shots, this antagonism. He's taunting the intelligence community.

> SENATOR SCHUMER: Let me tell you, you take on the intelligence community, they have six ways from Sunday at getting back at you. So, even for a practical, supposedly hard-nosed businessman, he's being really dumb to do this.

MADDOW: What do you think the intelligence community would do if they were—

SENATOR SCHUMER: I don't know. But from what I am told, they are very upset with how he has treated them and talked about them. And we need the intelligence community. We don't know what's going to— look at the Russian hacking. Without the intelligence community, we wouldn't have discovered it.

MADDOW: Do you think he has an agenda to dismantle parts of the intelligence community? This form of taunting hostile—

SENATOR SCHUMER: Let me tell you, whether you're a super liberal Democrat or a very conservative Republican, you should be against dismantling the intelligence community.[156]

For many observers this sounded like an implicit threat from Senator Schumer.

The question we ask in this book is: How many members of the intelligence community are working at CNN, and how many were in a position to have carried out such threats?

The answer is: more than you might imagine.

*** 

Our investigations, which include screen captures of all the information we discuss, and accessed through legal means, suggest that seventeen CNN employees are also members of the intelligence community, three CNN employees have worked at the White House in addition to being connected to the intelligence community, and one CNN employee worked first for the network as an intern, left to be employed by the intelligence community, then returned to CNN.

This means there are at least twenty-one CNN employees with ties to the intelligence community.

In the past, the intelligence agencies reached out to establish relationships with members of the press, eventually numbering more than four hundred such relationships. While we do not know if that program continues, it does appear that a new strategy has been deployed. That strategy involves directly placing members of the intelligence community into a media outlet. We have identified seventeen individuals who fit this profile.

Sometimes these individuals will have also worked at the White House, placing them in close proximity to the president and his team, presumably where advantageous ties could be established. We have identified three individuals who fit this profile.

Finally, the use of a former CNN intern, who was subsequently attached to an intelligence agency, then returned to CNN, also suggests that there is a short-, medium-, and long-range strategy employed by the intelligence agencies to influence the public.

## CNN Employees with Intelligence Backgrounds:

**Bianca Nobilo**—This CNN employee hosts *The Global Brief with Bianca Nobilo*, which airs on CNN International from Monday to Friday, at 5 p.m. ET.[157] Her CNN profile notes that:

> As a politics producer, Nobilo was heavily involved in CNN's political coverage planning and newsgathering. In 2017 she covered the Westminster terror attack, London Bridge terror attack, British General Election, OPEC summits and the triggering of Article 50.

> Nobilo has also secured exclusive interviews with IMF Managing Director Christine Lagarde and the Lebanese Minister for Foreign Affairs. Additionally, she interviewed George Osborne on the election of

President Trump and the architect of Brexit, Nigel Farage, in the lead up to the UK Brexit referendum. She also interviewed London mayor Sadiq Khan in the wake of the Parsons Green attack.

Furthermore, Nobilo produced both the inaugural CNN Middle East Business Forum in Abu Dhabi and the CNN Asia Business Forum in Bangalore.[158]

Nobilo has been a busy woman. Her CNN profile further boasts that she "holds a first-class degree in History from the University of Warwick, a Master of Science in Comparative Politics at the London School of Economics, where she specialized in conflict," and that "prior to working at CNN, Nobilo worked in the Houses of Parliament and in the defence and security sectors."[159] Just a cursory glance at her profile gives the impression she has friends in politics, the defense industry (intelligence agency aligned), and the media.

However, the information in her profile doesn't tell the whole story.

According to her LinkedIn page, from 2008 to 2012 she worked for Ashbourne Strategic Consulting Limited as a defense and security analyst.[160] Ashbourne is a third-party government contractor, which means that in order to do such work, Bianca would have had to obtain a security clearance, tying her to the intelligence services of Great Britain. From that job, Bianca went to work at the House of Commons as a senior political researcher.

This background is generally what is known as an "official cover" for intelligence members, as they can cite their security clearance as the reason for their association with intelligence officials.

**Bob Ortega**—Ortega is a senior writer for CNN Investigates, covering border and immigration issues.[161] Ortega's long history in journalism, an undergraduate degree from Princeton University, and a graduate degree from Columbia University's Graduate School of Journalism would seem to preclude any intelligence ties. His CNN profile states:

Ortega comes to CNN after a long career as an investigative journalist, most recently spending nearly six years at the Arizona Republic as a specialty writer covering the border and focusing on child welfare. He also served as managing editor for the Honolulu Civil Beat, which focuses on accountability journalism.[162]

Ortega's profile also highlights his various journalism awards but curiously omits the year and seven months (January 2009 to July 2010) he spent as vice consul of the US consulate in Guayaquil, Ecuador.[163] The job of a vice consul puts him under the authority of the State Department and would require him to obtain a security clearance, with a continuing legal obligation to the United States government not to divulge secrets. It's a curious position for a journalist.

It is also common for intelligence agents to be placed in diplomatic positions as "official cover" for an intelligence agency, providing them with diplomatic immunity if they are caught spying by the host country, requiring that at most they be deported, rather than being prosecuted.

**Jim Sciutto**—Sciutto is well-known to American audiences as the chief national security correspondent for CNN, as well as an anchor. His CNN page states that he is a "graduate of Yale University, where he studied Chinese history and was a Fulbright Fellow in Hong Kong. He is a member of the Council on Foreign Relations and an associate fellow at Pierson College at Yale."[164] He has also won Emmy Awards, the Edward R. Murrow Award, the George Polk Award, and the White House Correspondence Association's Merriman Smith Award for excellence in presidential coverage.[165]

With all this success in journalism, it's curious that he'd jump from the media to one of the most sensitive positions in all of diplomacy, chief of staff at the US embassy in Beijing, as he did from December 2011 to May 2013, a period of one year and six months.[166] His LinkedIn page describes him as "Chief of Staff and Senior Advisor to

Ambassador Gary Locke,"[167] which means he would have been privy to the most secret information held by the State Department.

Perhaps Sciutto took this job out of a sense of patriotic duty; and yet, the job would require him to obtain the highest level of security clearances, which in effect means that he may write only what the intelligence community allows him to write.

It is difficult to view Sciutto as anything other than an active asset of the intelligence agencies.

**Josh Campbell**—Campbell has been a correspondent at CNN since February 2018, and before that was an adjunct senior fellow at the Center for a New American Security (CAS), and from January 2019 to December 2019 was an adjunct professor at the University of Southern California.[168] This is a similar pattern to that of intelligence agents, who often go from private think tanks to academia, in addition to government work, and the new apparent destination, the mainstream media.

In his four years at CNN, Campbell has achieved a remarkable string of successes, covering some of the most controversial stories of the time. As stated on his CNN profile page:

> Campbell won an Emmy in 2021 for team coverage on the ground in Minnesota reporting on the murder of George Floyd, and continued to break news in the prosecution of the officers charged in his death. He reported from inside the courthouse as the verdict was read in the trial of the convicted senior police officer.
>
> His work also gained an Emmy nomination for team coverage of terrorism in America, and he contributed to CNN's award-winning team coverage on the ground in Istanbul following the murder of journalist Jamal Khashoggi.[169]

The most curious part of his LinkedIn page is where he describes the period from 2005 to 2018, thirteen years during which he was a "Supervisory Special Agent" for the Federal Bureau of Investigation (FBI).[170] Unlike for many other employees, CNN proudly lists these possible intelligence (likely CIA) associations in his CNN profile:

> Campbell joined CNN following a career in national security as a senior special agent with the FBI, conducting terrorism, cyber, and counterintelligence investigations. His work includes numerous anti-terrorism, post-blast, and hostage recovery operational deployments to conflict zones as a member of the FBI's global response force; diplomatic postings to American embassies abroad; crisis communication liaison to the White House and National Security Council; and Special Assistant to the Director of the FBI.[171]

It is the opinion of our investigators that, given the various roles in which Campbell has worked, he is most likely a CIA special embed to the FBI and is likely still a CIA asset as a CNN correspondent.

**Nicholas Best**—Since September 2021, Nicholas has been a senior producer for *Don Lemon Tonight*.[172] Best has worked for CNN since July 2013, first as an associate producer at CNN International; then, from December 2013 to November 2015, as a writer for CNN International; from November 2015 to March 2018 as a full producer for CNN International; from April 2018 to July 2019 as a senior producer for CNN International in Hong Kong; and as a producer for *Don Lemon Tonight* from July 2019 to August 2021.[173]

One might look at this résumé and conclude that there are no intelligence associations with which to be concerned.

However, Best's LinkedIn page includes the following account of his work as an Executive Office intern for US Ambassador Robert Tuttle from October 2008 to December 2008:

> Served as an intern in the Executive Office of Ambassador Robert H. Tuttle at the U.S. Embassy in London. Tracked and disseminated the highest level of classified documents. Researched for Embassy reports and correspondence.
>
> I helped plan, manage, and execute the Embassy's 2008 Election Night event, hosting over 2,000 people from politics and private industry.[174]

A public admission of handling "classified documents" is often used as a way of informing other intelligence professionals that this intelligence community member has "official cover."

It appears that Best became an intern for the State Department shortly after graduating from the Georgia Institute of Science, where he received a bachelor's of science. This would be consistent with a common intelligence agency practice of recruiting a promising asset during graduate or undergraduate studies.

**Kimberly Dozier**—Since July 2014, Dozier has been a global affairs analyst for CNN.[175] Since May 2019 she's also been a contributor to *Time* magazine, and since September 2021 she's been a visiting fellow at the Observer Research Foundation America.[176] Her personal website states:

> Career highlights include: 17 years as an award-winning CBS News foreign and national security correspondent; covering intelligence and counterterrorism for The Associated Press; national security for The Daily Beast; London bureau chief for CBS Radio

News; and executive editor of the intelligence-focused media startup The Cipher Brief.[177]

One can see a long and distinguished career in journalism, and yet from August 2014 to July 2015 there's a curious detour, as she became a full-time instructor at the US Army War College, holding the General Omar Bradley Chair in Strategic Leadership.[178]

In her description of this year on her LinkedIn page, she wrote:

- First woman awarded one-year chair shared by the Army War College, Dickinson School of Law, and Penn State University's Dickinson School of Law & School of International Affairs.
- Created and taught seminar on how news coverage impacts national security policy, from the Vietnam War to the Snowden leaks, for three audiences: college students; law students; and mid-career military officers and diplomats.[179]

It's genuinely puzzling why any of the investigative journalists of the 1960s and 1970s would have consented to teach military officers and diplomats about how journalism can affect their jobs. Many would find it difficult to imagine members of the media and the military, as well as diplomats (undercover intelligence officers?), sharing a faculty lounge.

The opinion of our investigators is that upon being appointed to her position at the US Army War College, Dozier would have likely received at least a "Secret" clearance from the Office of Personnel Management, as well as a National Agency Check with Local Agency Checks and Credit Check (NACLC) background check.

After that she would have been considered a de facto member of the intelligence community.

**Juliette Kayyem**—Kayyem is a national security, intelligence, and terrorism analyst for CNN, and arguably has the clearest ties to intelligence sources given the various jobs she has held in her career, including from 2007 to 2009 as the undersecretary of Homeland Security for the Commonwealth of Massachusetts, and from 2009 to 2010 as the assistant secretary for Intergovernmental Affairs at the US Department of Homeland Security.[180]

Her LinkedIn page notes that she has been a security analyst for CNN since 2013, and some might say she was even teasing her intelligence connections with *The SCIF Podcast* she's hosted since November 2016.[181] A sensitive compartmented information facility (SCIF) is usually an enclosed area in a building that is used to process sensitive compartmented information (SCI). Access to SCIFs is normally limited to those with the appropriate security clearances. Kayyem's own website states:

> In government, academia, journalism, and the private sector, Juliette Kayyem has served as a national leader in America's homeland security efforts....
>
> Kayyem appears frequently on CNN as their on-air national security analyst....
>
> A graduate of Harvard College and Harvard Law School, and the mother of three children, she is married to First Circuit Court of Appeals Judge David Barron.[182]

Government, academia, and journalism are all areas in which the intelligence agencies like to maintain a presence. The language of her LinkedIn descriptions of her work as the undersecretary of Homeland Affairs for Massachusetts, as well as being the assistant secretary for intergovernmental affairs for the US Department of Homeland Security, hint at these intelligence connections. From her LinkedIn page:

> The Office of Intergovernmental Affairs (IGA) promotes an integrated national approach to homeland

security by coordinating and advancing federal interaction with state, local, tribal, and territorial (SLTT)
governments. IGA is responsible for opening the
homeland security dialogue with executive-level part-
ners at the SLTT levels, along with the national associations representing them.[183]

Given her high-level positions in state and federal government,
with specific responsibility for protecting the country, it is inconceiv-
able that she would not be closely connected with, and obedient to,
US intelligence agencies. These positions would likely signal her official cover to other members of the intelligence community.

On February 10, 2022, Kayyem found herself in the news again
after her tweet about the Canadian truckers who were protesting
COVID-19 restrictions by blocking the parliament in Ottawa and
bridge crossings with the US. She wrote:

> The convoy protest, applauded by right wing media as
> a "freedom protest," is an economic and security issue
> now. The Ambassador Bridge link constitutes 28%
> of annual trade movement between US and Canada.
> Slash the tires, empty the gas tanks, arrest the drivers,
> and move the trucks.[184]

Many on Twitter criticized Kayyem for her effort to inflame ten-
sions, as well as to incite theft and destruction of property (a single
truck tire can cost hundreds of dollars), and a few hours later she was
back demanding even stronger reprisals:

> Trust me, I will not run out of ways to make this hurt:
> cancel their insurance; suspend their drivers' licenses;
> prohibit any future regulatory certification for truck-
> ers, etc. Have we learned nothing? These things fester
> when there are no consequences.[185]

In light of her Ivy League education and her work with the government, supposedly for the public good, it seems remarkable that she was suggesting a course of action that could only escalate the dispute.

**Melanie Lawrence**—Lawrence currently serves as the senior manager for security intelligence at WarnerMedia. Her LinkedIn pages shows she received a master's degree in clinical psychology from the Chicago School of Professional Psychology in 2007, then received an additional master's degree in strategic intelligence from the National Intelligence University (NIU) in 2010.[186]

The NIU website details some of its history:

> In August 1961, the Department of Defense established the Defense Intelligence Agency (DIA). DIA was responsible to the Joint Chiefs of Staff (JCS) for the integration of Department of Defense Intelligence and counterintelligence training programs, and career development of intelligence personnel. The Office of the Secretary of Defense (OSD) saw the logic and economy of consolidating duplicative strategic intelligence schools, and in February 1962, issued a memorandum directing the creation of a Defense Intelligence School.[187]

Let's just call it what it is: a school for intelligence agents, whether they're in the CIA, the Department of Defense, the Department of State, the National Security Agency, or the FBI.

And how did its name change from Defense Intelligence School to National Intelligence University? The website explains that as well.

> In December 2006, DoD Instruction 3305.1 changed our name to the National Defense Intelligence College. The DoD instruction was revised again in February 2011 to reflect the current designation—National

Intelligence—and the Director of National Intelligence formally and publicly announced that change as well as the expanded mission of the NIU during the August 2011 convocation to the class of 2012.[188]

If you're in charge of a major media organization and want to make sure it's being run by competent intelligence professionals, you might want a graduate of the National Intelligence University. And maybe you might want to make sure that this individual has not just academic skills, but has demonstrated his competence in the real world.

On her LinkedIn profile, Lawrence notes she was a "Psychometrist" in private practice from June 2007 to June 2009.[189] For those unfamiliar with the job of a psychometrist, here's a job description from a popular health website: "Psychometrists administer and score neuropsychological, psychological, personality and academic tests for patients with mild to severe traumatic brain injury, neurological diseases, psychological health issues or learning disabilities, or for psychological or neuropsychological research."[190]

After working as a psychometrist for two years, Lawrence became a "Defense Intelligence Scholar" at the US Department of Defense (DOD) from 2009 to 2010, then became an "Intelligence Analyst–Counterterrorism" at the DOD from 2010 to 2014.[191]

Lawrence's ties to the intelligence community seem self-evident, and the question must be asked why she has such an important position in a media company, if not to benefit the intelligence agencies, rather than the public.

**Cedric Leighton**—Leighton currently serves as a military analyst for CNN, and his associations include the National Security Agency as well as Air Force Intelligence. This is from the website for Cedric Leighton Associates that describes his work as an intelligence agent:

Cedric honed his analytical and leadership skills during a 26-year career as an intelligence officer in the U.S. Air Force. He witnessed the fall of the Berlin Wall, oversaw critical Special Operations missions, established key partnerships with nations in South and Southeast Asia and deployed five times to the Middle East. He served at every command echelon from small deployed elements to the Joint Staff at the Pentagon, where he was the Deputy Director for Warfighter Support and Integration in the Intelligence Directorate. His last military assignment was the National Security Agency's Deputy Director for Training....

He is a National Journal "National Security Insider," one of 89 nationally recognized experts who contribute insights every week.[192]

According to his LinkedIn profile, in 1984 he took both an "Air Force Basic Intelligence Officer Course" and an "Air Force Signals Intelligence Officer Course." From August 2000 to June 2001, he was chief of the Air Force's Congressional Affairs Branch, and from June 2001 to January 2003 he was the director of operations for the 70th Intelligence Wing at Fort Meade in Maryland.[193] He finished his Air Force career in July 2010 as deputy training director for the National Security Agency.[194]

In his twenty-six-year, career Leighton has held many positions, attesting to the fact he is highly intelligent and a smooth operator. He is the type of person who makes others feel comfortable and would be a powerful voice for any message an agency wanted to bring to the public.

**Amber Benjamin**—Benjamin currently serves as the director of Global Security Intelligence at WarnerMedia.[195] She has worked at

WarnerMedia since May 2020. Her employment history may be the most interesting of all twenty-one individuals profiled in this book, as it suggests a coordinated plan among the intelligence agencies, big tech, and the media.

On her LinkedIn page she states she was an intelligence analyst for the US Army from October 2005 to January 2010, a senior analyst for the CIA from June 2010 to December 2015, a supervisor for the Intelligence Program at the Department of Homeland Security from November 2015 to January 2019, and an intelligence analyst for Facebook from January 2019 until March 2020.[196]

It can be hard to believe that somebody would list her CIA employment on LinkedIn.

But we have the screen shot to prove it.

The work with Facebook is also extremely suggestive of an attempt to coordinate an approved intelligence message across several platforms.

**Andre Lawrence**—Lawrence has served as manager for quality assurance for the video platform for WarnerMedia since March 2020.[197] He has been at WarnerMedia for nine years, working as quality-assurance lead Direct to Consumer from March 2013 to March 2021.[198]

Prior to his work at WarnerMedia, he served as an intelligence analyst for the US Army from October 2009 to August 2019, which he described as "Us[ing] information derived from intelligence disciplines to determine changes in enemy capabilities, vulnerabilities, and probable courses of action."[199]

The information that Lawrence provides on his LinkedIn page is troubling, as it suggests that he was working for the US Army as an intelligence analyst *while* he was working for WarnerMedia.

We do not have an explanation for this apparent anomaly, other than to suggest he must have obtained some type of waiver from the US Army.

**Andrew McCabe**—McCabe was the second-highest-ranked individual in the FBI during the early part of the Trump presidency,[200] second only to James Comey and, later, Christopher Wray. He currently works at CNN as a senior law enforcement analyst, a position he has held since July 2019.[201]

It is important to realize that in his position as the second-highest-ranking official at the FBI, he would have been in charge of what are termed "official cover" (OC) and "non-official cover" (NOC) intelligence assets. An "asset" is usually defined as a clandestine source or method used for intelligence collection. He would also have been responsible for the assets' "handlers," who would issue "priority intelligence requirements" (PIRs) that give direction to the OC and NOC assets.

While most Americans think of the FBI as a law enforcement organization, they fail to realize that it is also an intelligence agency. McCabe's own LinkedIn account of his time at the FBI demonstrates the bureau's intelligence portion:

> In the final two years of a 21year career, I served as the FBI's second highest ranking leader, *overseeing all intelligence collection* and investigative operations, managing a workforce of 36,000 professionals and a budget of over $9 billion.[202] (Emphasis added.)

The employment background of Andrew McCabe might be more impressive, and of greater interest to CNN, had the FBI's inspector general not found McCabe guilty of lying under oath. From the April 13, 2018, *Washington Post*:

> The Justice Department Inspector General alleges in a damaging report made public Friday that former Deputy Director Andrew McCabe inappropriately authorized the disclosure of sensitive information to a reporter and then misled investigators and former

FBI Director James B. Comey about it on several occasions....

It accuses McCabe of lying at least four times, three of them under oath, and says that while he had the power to approve disclosures of information to the media, his doing so in this instance violated policy because it was done "in a manner designed to advance his personal interests at the expense of Department leadership."[203]

One would think that CNN would like to have a legal analyst who had not been found guilty of lying four times in an internal report by the FBI inspector general. As Trump was still in the midst of the "Russia collusion" story when this report was released, it's perhaps not surprising that he took some satisfaction in its findings. As the *Washington Post* reported:

Release of the report comes at a moment when the Justice Department and FBI are under intense scrutiny from a president upset that agents this week raided the office of his personal lawyer. McCabe had already alleged that his firing was politically motivated, as the president had made clear that he disliked McCabe long before the FBI's former No. 2 official was fired.

Trump wrote on Twitter Friday, "DOJ just issued the McCabe report—which is a total disaster. He LIED! LIED! LIED! McCabe was totally controlled by Comey—McCabe is Comey!! No collusion, all made up by this den of thieves and lowlifes!"[204]

This combination of an intelligence official who once wielded enormous power, and a reckless disregard for the truth, is one of the most powerful pieces of evidence that CNN is not engaged in traditional journalism.

**Arnaud Siad**—Siad currently works as a journalist and producer for CNN International.[205] His LinkedIn profile suggests three different possible associations with foreign intelligence agencies, most likely French:

(1) "Policy Analyst" for the North Atlantic Treaty Organization (NATO) from March of 2012 to September of 2012. "As a policy analyst at NATO, I was tasked with providing data support to the General Commander's team and help with the media campaign in the lead to the Chicago Summit of 2012. I drafted articles that were later published in *The New York Times* and *Le Monde*...."

(2) "Commercial Attaché" for French Embassy in Iceland from September 2009 to September 2010. "Provided the French Ambassador with weekly reports on the economic and financial developments in post-crisis Iceland [2009 collapse of the home mortgage market] and covered the Icesave dispute for the Embassy."

(3) "Managing Director" of the French-Icelandic Chamber of Commerce, Minister of the Economy, Industry and Employment (France)—Also from September 2009 to September 2010. "The French-Icelandic Chamber of Commerce is tasked with providing support to French and Icelandic businesses seeking to invest and/or increase their presence in both markets."[206]

The contemporary French intelligence and counterintelligence system can be confusing, but some historical perspective will lend clarity. Siad worked for both the Ministry of Economy and Finance and the French diplomatic corps as a commercial attaché at the French embassy in Iceland. His work at such a high level in the diplomatic corps would have likely given him "official cover" as an intelligence asset, while his work with the French-Icelandic Chamber of Commerce, under the minister of the Economy, Industry and Employment, would have provided him with "non-official cover."

By becoming a policy analyst at NATO, it is likely that his work in intelligence had become solid enough to earn a promotion to the French intelligence position as a commercial attaché at the French embassy before joining CNN International.

Our opinion is that Arnaud Siad is likely a foreign intelligence service operative, and his employment by CNN raises questions about CNN's journalistic objectivity.

**Pete Licata**—Licata has been under contract with CNN as a law enforcement analyst since November 2020, according to his LinkedIn profile.[207]

From April 1992 until September 1999 he was a commissioned officer in the US Army, a "paratrooper, Ranger qualified, 82nd Airborne, 10th Mountain division," as well as having "served on General Staff as the Intelligence Operations Officer."[208] From the US Army he moved to the FBI where he worked from September 1999 to October 2020 as a supervisory special agent/team leader where he "directed federal criminal investigations with an emphasis on domestic and international terrorism."[209] Again, in order to perform this work he would have needed security clearances—making him a member of the intelligence community.

Since October 2020, Licata has worked as the "Deputy Program Coordinator for Operations, Operation Somalia, Department of Justice" (in addition to his contract with CNN).[210] He describes this work as follows:

> Serves as second in command of a team of 25 advisors and staff providing advisement and subject matter expertise to the Somali Federal Police Force specializing in counterterrorism operations. Synchronizes

actions to achieve programmatic goals of a $20 million US government sponsored program.[211]

During his time in the US Army, Licata was an intelligence operations officer; during his time at the FBI, he worked on domestic and international terrorism, and in his new role for the Department of Justice he focuses on counterterrorism operations.

The evidence appears strong that Licata is an "official cover" intelligence asset and his use by CNN without disclosing this information is a disservice to its audience.

**Jamie Gangel**—The evidence for CNN special correspondent Jamie Gangel is less persuasive than the evidence for most of the individuals on this list. Her LinkedIn profile lists her places of education as The Dalton School, Harvard University, and the Georgetown University School of Foreign Service.[212] All three of these institutions have traditionally been known as places where the intelligence services recruit. A little background on The Dalton School will highlight these ties.

During World War II, Donald Barr—who would later become headmaster of The Dalton School in 1964, father of William Barr (US attorney general under Donald Trump), served in the Office of Strategic Services (OSS), the precursor to the CIA. William Barr would also work for the intelligence agencies. A 2019 *Vanity Fair* article covered some of the dual history of the elder and younger Barr regarding their work for the intelligence agencies.

On the subject of Donald Barr becoming headmaster of the elite Dalton School, *Vanity Fair* wrote:

> The son of an economist and a psychologist, he had attended New York's progressive Lincoln School in the 1930s and, in the style of the era, was a Marxist, then a fierce anti-Communist after World War II. Lincoln was a Valhalla of intellect where John D. Rockefeller Jr. sent his own children to learn with the new John

Dewey principles, which were geared toward each child's own strengths. During the war, Barr joined the OSS—forerunner to the CIA—and later taught English at Columbia, was an associate dean in the engineering school, and ran a weekend program for gifted high school students.[213]

So, we have Donald Barr, father of William Barr, the attorney general of the United States during the final years of the Trump presidency, working for the forerunner of the CIA. But William Barr, also worked for the intelligence agencies, specifically the CIA, which he hoped one day to head.[214] *Vanity Fair* detailed how a young William Barr navigated the tumultuous Sixties:

> In the face of all this turbulence, Barr went to Columbia, which erupted his freshman year. The campus strikes and shutdowns, he would later admit, were absolutely crucial in focusing his priorities. When student protests shuttered college buildings, he used the word anarchic to describe the face-off, furious that the demonstrators—with whom he tangled at the time—were interfering with his ability to enter the library for his classwork in Chinese studies.
>
> Soon after graduation, Barr joined the CIA as a China analyst while attending George Washington law at night and married Christine Moynihan, a librarian.[215]

We have a young William Barr as a young China scholar, working for the CIA, while he's going to law school at night. What might Barr's duties have entailed while working at the CIA? One article, released around the time Trump nominated him for attorney general described Barr's likely work at the CIA as follows:

Barr is the spawn of the last Cold Warriors, an infinitely powerful group of affluent white men who dominated the U.S. intelligence apparatus for four decades. He was assigned to the China Desk, a rookie working for America's greatest spooks who were busy running numerous "black" Southeast Asian operations.

The China Desk's biggest job in the early 1970s was the Vietnam War's "Phoenix" program, an effort to murder South Vietnamese who ran afoul of the U.S.-installed regime. Another was the CIA-run Golden Triangle narco-trafficking enterprise that helped create a generation of American junkies comprised of soldiers who succumbed to white powder's sublime calling.[216]

Jamie Gangel has certainly had many opportunities to be recruited into the intelligence services, given her attendance at the Dalton School, Harvard University, and Georgetown university, all well-known recruitment centers for the intelligence agencies. She would have been identified as a likely target for recruitment, given her interest in journalism. The same skills a journalist employs in getting people to talk is also an important asset for an intelligence agent.

However, in fairness it must be said the evidence for her actual recruitment is only circumstantial at this time.

**Calvin Sims**—Sims is executive vice president of standards and practices at CNN.[217] His likely tie to the intelligence community comes from his membership as a senior fellow at the Council on Foreign Relations (CFR) from September 2001 until February 2003.[218] This is how Sims describes his work for the CFR on LinkedIn:

Appointed Senior Fellow at the Council on Foreign Relations. Led research project that examined the rise of radical Islamic forces in Indonesia. Coedited online encyclopedia on terrorism for the Council's website. Awarded the Council's Edward R. Murrow Press Fellowship. Conducted professional training workshops and cultural exchange programs for journalists in Turkey, Armenia, and Azerbaijan as part of an effort to resolve historical conflicts with American University's Center for Global Peace.[219]

The CFR is a US State Department think tank and news source, and work by its members often appears in *Foreign Affairs* and *Foreign Policy*. Many consider these publications to be tools of politically motivated intelligence collectors and researchers, providing policy makers with an independent stamp of approval for decisions that are secretly being made by the intelligence agencies. The CFR is well known as a recruiting base for the US State Department. It is also common for senior intelligence members to work at this supposedly independent think tank when their parties aren't in political power. This allows them the freedom to be available for any presidential appointments, especially if a political party is in trouble and may select an expert from the supposedly opposite side of the ideological spectrum to appear bipartisan.

Our researchers consider this individual's association with the Council on Foreign Relations as giving him "official cover" as a member of the intelligence community.

**Fareed Zakaria**—Zakaria is well known to CNN viewers as the host of *Fareed Zakaria GPS*, which is described in his CNN profile page as a "television destination for global newsmakers, U.S. politicians, CEOs, and thought-leading authors and journalists."[220] His CNN profile also describes Zakaria's importance in global affairs:

Zakaria has won numerous awards and been named to various lists, including Foreign Policy magazine's list of "Top 100 Global Thinkers" and Newsweek magazine's "Power 50" list of the most influential political figures of 2010. In 1999, Esquire magazine named Zakaria as "One of the 21 Most Important People of the 21st Century."

He serves on the boards of Yale University, the Council on Foreign Relations, the Trilateral Commission, and Shakespeare and Company, a theater group in the Berkshires. He has received honorary degrees from Brown, the University of Miami, and Oberlin College, among other educational institutions.

Zakaria earned a bachelor's degree from Yale University and a doctorate in political science from Harvard University.[221]

The pattern of associations, from the praise of mainstream publications to Ivy League universities, as well as his work with the Council on Foreign Relations and the Trilateral Commission, all point to intelligence ties.

And just so you don't think he's all work and no play, he belongs to a theater group!

Zakaria's LinkedIn profile also suggests two other possible intelligence ties. First, from 1991 to 1992 he was director of the CSE Project at Harvard University's Center for International Affairs, and second, from 1992 to 2000 he was the editor of *Foreign Affairs* magazine.[222]

Harvard is well-known as a CIA recruiting location, and the fact that Zakaria was invited back to teach at the Harvard Center for International Affairs is also evidence of a CIA connection.

*Foreign Affairs* is one of the most highly respected "open-source" intelligence publications oriented toward State Department employees, and is also believed to be a primary source used by overseas "non-official cover" intelligence operatives.

In his role as a CNN host, Zakaria has a plausible reason to meet with highly placed foreign dignitaries as well as members of the US intelligence community.

## CNN Employees with Intelligence Ties and White House Experience

An intelligence agent placed inside a media organization will have a certain value. But that value is likely to be significantly higher if the agent has also worked in the White House and developed relationships with long-term staff, who are able to keep the agent informed of current happenings inside 1600 Pennsylvania Avenue.

We have identified three individuals who fit this profile.

**Anthony J. Ferrante**—Ferrante has been a national security analyst for CNN since January 2019. His intelligence background is clear to anybody who might happen upon his résumé at Forensic Technologies International (FTI) Consulting:

> Prior to joining FTI Consulting, Mr. Ferrante served as Director for Cyber Incident Response at the U.S. National Security Council at the White House where he coordinated U.S. response to unfolding domestic and international cybersecurity crises and issues. Building on his extensive cybersecurity and incident response experience, he led the development and implementation of Presidential Policy Directive 41— United States Cyber Incident Coordination, the federal government's national policy guiding cyber incident response efforts.

Before joining the National Security Council, Mr. Ferrante was Chief of Staff of the FBI's Cyber Division. He joined the FBI as a special agent in 2005, assigned to the FBI's New York Field Office. In 2006, Mr. Ferrante was selected as a member of the FBI's Cyber Action Team, a fly-team of experts who deploy globally to respond to the most critical cyber incidents on behalf of the U.S. government.[223]

Ferrante held the position of "Director for Cyber Incident Response" from October 2015 to April 2017,[224] which would have covered the 2016 election when Candidate Trump was supposedly soliciting help from the Russian government. It is clear from the start of Ferrante's career at the FBI that he was focusing on international issues, and his clear bias would have been to present information in a way that was acceptable to the bureaucracies he served, rather than the more impartial standards of journalism. His pattern of work would have likely given him "official cover" as an intelligence asset, meaning that he was somebody with whom other assets could communicate openly.

However, this leaves his work at CNN as a national security analyst open to suspicion that his true motive does not involve informing the public.

**Shawn Turner**—Turner also works at CNN as a national security analyst, and his work history may be the most troubling regarding where his true allegiances lie—with the public or the with intelligence agencies he once served. His White House service is also of great concern.

According to his LinkedIn profile, Turner was the deputy White House press secretary from June 2014 to June 2015.[225] He described his duties as "responsible for engaging members of the news media on issues related to U.S. national security and homeland security issues."[226]

From May 2011 until May 2014, Turner was the director of Public Affairs, US National Intelligence, at the Office of the Director of National Intelligence.[227] He wrote: "Director of Public Affairs for U.S. National Intelligence responsible for coordinating and overseeing the communication efforts of the 16 U.S. intelligence agencies and components."[228] I'll bet you didn't know there were sixteen US intelligence agencies, in addition to the Office of the Director of National Intelligence. It kind of makes you wonder what they're all doing.

From July 2010 until May 2011, Turner was the assistant press secretary for foreign affairs at the White House, which he described as "Director of communication and outreach for Afghanistan, Pakistan, and North Africa."[229] Again, there is no way to describe this position as being anything other than an intelligence asset.

From June 2009 to July 2010, he worked at the "OSD [Office of the Secretary of Defense] Public Affairs Office, Central Command, Middle East, Department of Defense."[230]

Can CNN genuinely believe that this person will give independent advice, with two positions in the White House, in addition to what must have been the highest of security clearances in order to work with the "16 U.S. intelligence agencies and components?"

Turner's biography at the George Washington School of Media and Public Affairs, where he now teaches, has these highlights:

> Shawn Turner is the on-air national security and communications analyst and the former chair of the Information Operations Department at Daniel Morgan Graduate School of National Security (DMGS). While at DMGS, Turner taught graduate courses on information and decision making, as well as courses on the use of disinformation as an instrument of national power....
>
> In 2013, he was the lead government official responsible for engaging news media organizations after the

removal of thousands of classified intelligence documents by NSA [National Security Agency] contractor,
Edward Snowden.

At the White House and NSC [National Security
Council], he was the principal spokesperson for U.S.
Foreign Policy in Afghanistan and Pakistan, and
helped develop the government's approach to com-
municating intelligence reform in 2014....

In recent years, Turner was named one of Washington
D.C.'s top decision makers by the National Journal
(2013), honored with the Intelligence Community
Leadership Award (2015) and in 2016, he was
awarded the Meritorious Presidential Rank Award for
outstanding career accomplishments and exemplary
service to the nation.[231]

For most traditional journalists, awards by the government are
not a badge of honor and would generally raise suspicion. Turner may
have earned his 2013 "Intelligence Community Leadership Award,"
but that would not have inspired respect among the media of the past.

**Rodney Hirsch**—Hirsch was a Secret Service agent for many high-
profile Republicans and now works as the assistant security manager
for WarnerMedia.

From May 2008 to October 2015, he was assigned to protect
Republican Speaker of the House Paul Ryan, in June 2012 he was the
lead emergency vehicle operator/intelligence officer for the Romney-
Ryan 2012 presidential campaign, and from 2016 to 2017 he was
assigned to protect Republican Senator Ron Johnson.[232] Protection
of leading politicians routinely involves handling of classified
information.

From February 2017 until October 2017, Hirsch worked as an "Executive Protection Agent" for executives at Lockheed-Martin, one of the country's leading defense contractors, with which the US government shares a great deal of top-secret information. Of this job, Hirsch wrote on LinkedIn: "Provided Executive protection to CEO, President and Chairman of the Board. Conduct advance site surveys, secure transportation, U.S. and overseas travel. Safeguard Top Secret/classified information and material. Expanded detail provided per confidential specifications."[233] From October 2017 until September 2019, Hirsch served as a "Federal/National Security, Special Investigator," for Constellis in Reston, Virginia.[234] Constellis is a third-party government subcontractor to the US Office of Personnel Management.

Secret Service agents are normally directly involved in dignitary escort details and physical security, as well as white collar financial investigations. They are also often in direct contact with classified materials and often develop relationships with multiple administrations.

## CNN Intern Joins Intelligence Community, Then Returns to CNN

Bethany Crudele Jones—The employment history of Bethany Crudele Jones suggests a long-term strategy on the part of the intelligence agencies to embed friendly assets in the media, hoping that they forever blur the line between intelligence agent and media employee, regardless of the position they might hold. Perhaps the individual involved does not even realize that she or he is a friendly asset; it's just that she or he is very willing to accept the claims of current intelligence "friends" who always helpfully seem to have just the information needed for a story.

Jones began her career as an intern for the National Press Club in 2006, then worked for Democratic Senator Jack Reed from Rhode Island.[235] In 2007, she became an intern for CNN and in 2008 made the jump to become a "Foreign Disclosure Assistant at U.S. Marine Headquarters."[236] As Jones wrote in her LinkedIn profile:

- Tasks included matters related to foreign disclosure and technology transfer.
- Helped rewrite the official foreign disclosure/visits manual.
- Compiled the Commandant's Middle East trip books ahead of foreign visits.
- Drafted delegation of disclosure authority letters for foreign billets.
- Authored a treatise on the challenges of integrating political communication techniques during military operations.
- Administrative assistance and communication with foreign embassies.[237]

Let's discuss just a few of the tasks that Jones performed during her ten months at the US Marine Corps headquarters. She worked on "foreign disclosure and technology transfer," helped to rewrite the "official foreign disclosure/visits manual," assembled the "Commandant's Middle East trip books ahead of foreign visits," and wrote a "treatise on the challenges of integrating political communication techniques during military operations." [Authors' note: Is a "political communication technique," just another expression for "disinformation?"]

All these tasks require security clearances and security oaths. One should ask where her loyalties lie, with the community of journalism or the government agencies. In May 2009 she technically returned to journalism but remained at the Pentagon as a "Pentagon Unit Intern" for CNN.[238] From July 2012 until December 2012 she was a deputy news editor and reporter for the *Marine Corps Times*, then returned to CNN. In July 2021, she became a senior producer on *New Day Weekend with Christi Paul and Boris Sanchez* at CNN's headquarters in Atlanta.[239]

In addition, Jones attended the George Washington University School of Media and Public Affairs, a historically known intelligence recruitment institution. Our researchers believe that Bethany Crudele Jones has been given "official cover" as an intelligence community member and that her employment at CNN is suspect.

We worry that this case suggests that the intelligence agencies are targeting individuals at the beginning of their careers, employing them, then returning them to the media where they will either be sympathetic to, or take instruction from, the intelligence community in their reporting or in the production of shows for which they are responsible.

***

On February 6, 2018, Jack Shafer, senior media writer at *Politico*, wrote an article with the title "The Spies Who Came in to the TV Studio."[240] This was during the time that Cary was still employed at CNN, struggling with what he was seeing. In many ways, the article mirrors many of the concerns raised in this chapter. The article opened:

> In the old days, America's top spies would complete their tenure at the CIA or one of the other Washington puzzle palaces and segue to more ordinary pursuits. Some wrote their memoirs. One ran for president. Another died a few months after surrendering his post. But today's national security establishment retiree has a different game plan. After so many years of brawling in the shadows, he yearns for a second, lucrative career in the public eye. He takes a crash course in speaking in soundbites, refreshes his wardrobe and signs a TV news contract.[241]

It's instructive to realize that this article on spies in the newsroom came out just a little over two years after President Trump took the oath of office, almost exactly halfway in his term. The list of intelligence officials who were finding their way into the newsrooms of America was truly remarkable.

> Former CIA Director John Brennan (2013-17) is the latest superspook to be reborn as a TV newsie. He just cashed in at NBC News as a "senior national security and intelligence analyst" and served his first expert views on last Sunday's edition of *Meet the Press*. The Brennan acquisition seeks to elevate NBC to spook parity with CNN, which employs former Director of National Intelligence James Clapper and former CIA Director Michael Hayden in a similar capacity.[242]

Yes, it seems like there's a gold rush at all the networks to get these former spooks. But it's not just those at the top who seem to be in demand:

> Other, lesser-known national security veterans thrive under TV's grow lights. Almost too numerous to list, they include Chuck Rosenberg, former acting DEA administrator, chief of staff for FBI director James B. Comey, and counselor to former FBI Director Robert S. Mueller III; Frank Figliuzzi, former chief of FBI counterintelligence; Juan Zarate, deputy national security adviser under Bush, at CBS News. CNN's bulging roster also includes former FBI agent Asha Rangappa; former FBI agent James Gagliano; Obama's former deputy national security adviser Tony Blinken; former House Intelligence Committee Chairman Mike Rogers; senior adviser to the National Security Council during the Obama administration Samantha Vinograd; retired CIA operations officer Steven L. Hall; and Philip Mudd, also retired from the CIA.

And CNN is still adding to its bench. Last Saturday, former Comey aide Josh Campbell wrote a *New York Times* op-ed on why he was leaving the FBI on principle. By Monday, the network was announcing his new position as a "law enforcement analyst."[243]

But does the article miss what might actually be taking place? Are these intelligence officials simply pursuing a second career at the news networks? Or are they working as agents of disinformation at the networks as an extension of their first career?

As the John le Carré wrote in his novel *A Perfect Spy*, beloved by longtime Reagan CIA chief William Casey, "In every operation there is an above the line and a below the line. Above the line is what you do by the book. Below the line is how you do the job."

Are the spies like John Brennan, James Clapper, and Michael Hayden who are working at the networks the "above the line" guys, while the twenty-one individuals we've identified as working at CNN are the "below the line" guys who "do the job?"

And does that job entail misleading the public and making us hate each other by claiming half the country is racist, hyping the Russia collusion story, calling for the impeachment of a president, and concealing the true origins of COVID-19, while they carry out their plans?

The concluding chapters of this book detail the possible motivations behind such plans.

# CHAPTER SEVEN

# Two Experts Weigh In
# on Our Claims

As we were finishing up this book, we sent a few relevant chapters to a former FBI agent who'd spent thirty-three years at the bureau, for his reaction. This agent had also served as the legal attaché in two Western capitals, jobs that required him to meet regularly with the local CIA chief of station, as well as lower-ranking CIA officials.

The former agent requested anonymity, and we granted his request. However, he had no objection to providing comments on background about questions we'd raised about intelligence agencies and the media.

The agent praised us for providing historical background on these questions and for grounding our claims in the protections granted by the Constitution.[244] The bias suggested by the social media contacts between CNN and the White House seemed to this agent to be well supported. Our agent was also puzzled by the large number of individuals working at CNN's Digital Intelligence Unit, as well as by the fact that several of them apparently had cyberwarfare skills. The report raised questions about what the Digital Intelligence Unit might attempt in the future.

The agent believed the statement by Senator Chuck Schumer in the days before President Trump took the oath of office was an important piece of evidence, giving the motive for the intelligence agencies to attack Trump with claims of phony Russian collusion. Schumer said that if you took on the intelligence agencies, they had "six ways from Sunday at getting back at you." Our agent believed this to be critical to understanding what happened in the four years of the Trump presidency.

The agent did warn us to be skeptical of some of the claims by CNN and WarnerMedia employees in their LinkedIn listings about the importance of their jobs and what they may have done. The agent was familiar with some of the FBI agents we listed who claimed intelligence backgrounds and thought our characterizations of them may have been mistaken. On the broader question, though, of how much the intelligence agencies were influencing the media, he thought that to be an extremely important inquiry, and one to which he, even at his level, did not have a clear answer.

The agent also provided some background on what he believed had gone wrong at the FBI in the past decades. In his opinion, the FBI changed dramatically under the reign of then-FBI Director Robert Mueller, when Mueller was tasked by President George W. Bush not only with finding those responsible for the terrorist attacks of 9/11, but also with *preventing* any additional similar attacks.

This changed the character of the FBI from a law enforcement entity to an intelligence agency, identifying and neutralizing domestic threats before they materialized. The agent was deeply troubled by this melding of the FBI into a law enforcement *and* intelligence agency. Having worked with various CIA chiefs of station in his foreign postings, the agent was well acquainted with the institutional differences between the FBI and the CIA.

In his estimation, working for the FBI as a traditional law enforcement agency, the FBI agent was always moving toward the moment where he would stand up in a court of law, raise his right hand, and swear to "tell the truth, the whole truth, and nothing but the truth."

By contrast, the CIA's covert mission required the use of deception and deceit. Even as the FBI attaché in foreign capitals, the agent had several instances in which he was lied to by his CIA counterpart, even when it was on a matter of little or no importance. The FBI and CIA representatives in these foreign countries were supposed to tell each other the truth. But the agent discovered he had been lied to on several key issues, such as whether certain State Department officials were working for the CIA as analysts. Once, a friendly Western government found the CIA was spying on it, and the agent was left to deal with the fallout from the furious government.

Of course, the CIA agents were not arrested, not even declared persona non grata, but simply allowed to quietly leave the country. The leadership of the FBI was furious when it found out what the CIA had done.

When the CIA station chief later brought up the issue with the FBI director and said it would have gone the same way had the FBI been doing something similarly illegal in the United States, the FBI director fixed him with a steely gaze and said the agents would have been "in handcuffs."

In his interactions with CIA personnel, the agent noted their propensity to lie, even about unimportant matters and even to an individual with whom they were supposed to be truthful. During a frank conversation with the local CIA chief of station, the agent was told that the habit of lying became so ingrained in many CIA personnel that the CIA leadership often had meetings with personnel to tell them they didn't have to lie about everything.

Andrew McCabe, the former deputy director of the FBI, came in for special criticism from the agent, as he felt McCabe did not follow the bureau's standard for honesty and should never have been hired by CNN. The FBI had fired McCabe for lying, and there had been a spirited debate inside the FBI about whether McCabe should be criminally prosecuted. Eventually, the decision was made not to prosecute McCabe.

Another problem raised by the retired agent is the question of what he called "circular reporting," in which a piece of intelligence is submitted by one agency, then simply repeated by the other agencies. Often this happens through simple human error, but it can also be caused by a devious single originator.

The agent named Andrew McCabe, Peter Strzok, and James Comey as the three greatest miscreants at the FBI. They showed no remorse for their actions, and it was their hubris that really got under the agent's skin.

The agent also identified John Brennan, former director of the CIA, and James Clapper, the former director of National Intelligence, as "the real devils" in what has gone on in this country over the past several years. In the opinion of the agent, Brennan carries himself with a certain gravitas, and it is understandable why people might believe him.

But Clapper seemed to be of low intelligence, simply blundering through one factual misstatement after another, often getting basic facts wrong, but never in doubt.

\*\*\*

Supporting these suspicions about CIA malfeasance is an article in the *Wall Street Journal* from August 5, 2018, by another retired FBI agent, Thomas J. Baker, who worked in a variety of investigative and management positions dealing with crime and terrorism. Baker asks how the Russia collusion investigation started and suggests what might have happened:

> Did the Central Intelligence Agency lead the Federal Bureau of Investigation down a rabbit hole in the counterintelligence investigation of Donald Trump's 2016 presidential campaign?

Although the FBI's case officially began July 31, 2016, there had been investigative activity before that date. John Brennan's CIA might have directed activity in Britain, which could be a problem because of long-standing agreements that the U.S. will not conduct intelligence operations there. It would explain why the FBI continues to stonewall Congress as to the inquiry's origin.[245]

This goes along with the statement from Senator Schumer about the intelligence agencies going after Trump because of his criticisms of their work. The intelligence agencies appear to have been targeting Trump through his 2016 run, even before his election. Baker states the appropriate standard for the instigation of an FBI case as being "predicate information," or "articulable facts," which was missing in the case against Trump:

> From what has been made public, all that passes for predicate information in this matter originated in Britain. Stephan Halper, an American who ran the Centre of International Studies at Cambridge, had been a CIA source in the past. Recent press reports describe him as an FBI informant. Joseph Misfud, another U.K.-based academic with ties to Western intelligence, met with Trump campaign aide George Papadopoulos on April 26, 2016. Mr. Misfud report-edly mentioned "dirt" on Hillary Clinton. Then, on May 10, Mr. Papadopoulos met with Australian Ambassador Alexander Downer in London, to whom he relayed the "dirt" on Mrs. Clinton.[246]

Stephen Halper, a CIA or FBI spook, depending on whom you believe.

Joseph Misfud, "connected" to Western intelligence.

The Australian ambassador, Alexander Downer. Do you really believe an ambassador doesn't have intelligence connections, especially with his American friends? Let's be real. Diplomats are often the "polite" spies, who, if caught, don't spend years in prison and are simply made to leave the country.

Does it seem like there were a lot of spooks trying to gain access to the Trump campaign? If they were hanging around a political campaign, how likely is it they'd hang around a news organization like CNN?

Inquiring minds want to know!

Baker continued:

> The FBI lacked any real predicate. But in the post-9/11 world, a referral from the CIA would cause some in the FBI to believe they had to act—particularly as the agency's information originated with America's closest ally. Shortly after the case opened that summer, Mr. Brennan gave a briefing to then-Senate Majority leader Harry Reid, telling him that the CIA had referred the matter to the FBI—an obvious effort to pressure the bureau to get moving on the collusion case.

> As the FBI's investigation progressed, it would use a surveillance warrant against Carter Page, a former member of Mr. Trump's campaign, who had been in contact with Mr. Halper. A dossier prepared for the Clinton campaign by Christopher Steele, formerly of Britain's MI6, was used to obtain the warrant.

> The existence of the investigation was withheld from the congressional "gang of eight" because of its "sensitivity," former FBI Director James Comey, later said.[247]

The coincidences just keep piling up. The author of the report that led to the Russia collusion investigation was a former British spy. And the official who kept this information from Congress was none other than FBI Director James Comey, whose agency now collects intelligence on American citizens, in addition to interacting with foreign intelligence services.

In a later article about how at least the FBI might be reformed, Baker advocated a return to constitutional principles, which the agency still followed when he joined:

> FBI special agents always have been instructed about the Constitution. But a new category of employee arose after 9/11. Intelligence analysts, who don't directly interact with citizens in ways that touch on the Constitution's guarantees, now play a major role in the bureau's mission. These employees deal in estimates and best guesses. Their actions also ultimately affect people's liberty. It is imperative that they, too, receive training about the Constitution.
>
> As former FBI Director William Webster repeatedly told us: "We must do the job the American people expect of us, in the way that the Constitution demands of us." All actions and decisions must once again be viewed through that prism.[248]

The way forward for both federal agencies and the media is clear. These are not new concept but rather long-established traditions. The media and the government are supposed to be at odds with each other.

That is the fundamental tension in our system of government, which keeps us free.

The public wants to ensure that actions taken in secret are eventually brought to light.

America's tradition is that of a truth-telling culture, and if we, as citizens, surrender it, we choose a dark and scary path.

However, the second expert who commented on this book paints an even more terrifying picture.

\*\*\*

If the anonymous FBI agent can be characterized as politically conservative, the second expert we consulted, long-time American constitutional trial lawyer Daniel Sheehan, was squarely in the liberal, even progressive, camp. Sheehan might accurately be described as America's most preeminent cause lawyer, having graduated from both Harvard Law and Harvard Divinity School.[249]

Sheehan litigated the Pentagon Papers case in 1971, the Watergate burglary in 1973, and in 1976 was the chief attorney on the Karen Silkwood case, investigating the mysterious death of the safety inspector for the Oil, Chemical, and Atomic Workers Union. His work in the Silkwood case revealed that the CIA's Israeli desk had been smuggling 98 percent bomb-grade plutonium to both Israel and Iran, led at that time by the shah. In 1984, Sheehan was chief trial counsel for the American sanctuary movement, protecting church workers who were trying to assist Central American refugees fleeing political violence in their home countries. This work led to the revelations in 1986 of the Iran-Contra scandal, in which it was shown that members of the Reagan administration were shipping weapons to the Nicaraguan Contras, in violation of Congress, then illegally shipping weapons to the Iranian mullahs in an ill-fated attempt to secure a diplomatic opening. Sheehan remains active in many current cases, working through his Romero Institute, a public interest law firm based on Catholic concepts of truth and justice.

When Kent raised the idea with Daniel that intelligence agencies were inserting themselves into CNN, he had a lot to say. He started with how he was one of the founders of the *Harvard Civil Rights Law Review* in 1968 and solicited cases from lawyers around the country.

(Sheehan graduated from Harvard Law School in 1970.) As an editor at the *Harvard Civil Rights Law Review*, he developed the case that established the right of journalists to protect their confidential news sources.

By working on that case, he made many friends with people in the news industry. He also began collaborating with a law firm that represented many news outlets, writing the briefs for cases involving NBC, CBS, ABC, the *New York Times*, and the *Washington Post*. It was in that capacity that he ended up being one of the four main lawyers on the Pentagon Papers case.

One of the arguments made by the Nixon administration was that the *New York Times* didn't have the right to decide which classified information it could publish. Sheehan responded by pointing out that the *New York Times* never took a security oath and also added an affidavit from Kennedy administration official Ted Sorensen about how he met regularly with the *New York Times* editorial board, briefing its members on covert operations. The *New York Times* would then decide which of these programs to cover, usually with permission from the administration.

When Sheehan saw this and other documents, he started to more deeply question how much the intelligence community, the government, and the media were working together. Eventually, Sheehan claims he discovered forty-two intelligence agents who were embedded in the major news media organizations he was representing.

This infiltration was later revealed to be part of a program called Operation Mockingbird.

Sheehan also claims that Ben Bradlee, the legendary editor of the *Washington Post*, was a long-time CIA guy. Philip Graham, the owner of the *Post*, was a full-time CIA agent, according to Sheehan. In fact, his widow, Katharine Graham, celebrated her eightieth birthday at CIA headquarters in Langley, Virginia.

The argument made by the intelligence agencies to these media outlets was that if they were going to have national security correspondents, it only made sense that these correspondents have good sources and contacts in the intelligence community.

Inevitably, that would mean that the national security correspondents would generally be members of the national intelligence community themselves.

However, in Sheehan's telling of the history, the intelligence community had many more members in the media than just among the ranks of the national security correspondents.

Sheehan told us that while he believed our investigation uncovered evidence of the intelligence agencies utilizing CNN, we weren't properly understanding the issue. We needed to understand that the titans of media in the late 1940s and early 1950s, people like William Paley of CBS and Henry Luce of *Time* magazine had already created the pipeline through which the views of the intelligence community would trump genuine investigative journalism. Especially if these investigations came too close to sensitive topics, such as the Kennedy assassination or the Phoenix assassination programs utilized during the Vietnam War. He also discussed how the CIA strategy of running guns to anti-communist rebels and in return bringing drugs back into the United States had been developed in the fight against Mao Tse Tung in China, and was later used during the Vietnam War and in Reagan's Central American efforts.

In a serendipitous turn of events, Sheehan revealed that he'd been a friend of CNN founder Ted Turner since 1978, even before the launch of CNN. At the time, Turner wanted to talk to Sheehan about what kind of programming the new network would run. Turner wanted a program like *Washington Week in Review* (which was then on PBS), but Sheehan suggested that rather than having on all these mouthpieces for the *New York Times*, *Time*, and *Newsweek*, CNN should have the heads of the public interest organizations, which were actually independent.

The idea came close to fruition but never materialized.

Sheehan remembered those as great times with Turner, eventually becoming so close to Ted that they'd often take a hot tub together, smoke a joint, and discuss the way the world really worked. Six years later, Sheehan found himself at Turner's house again, sitting in the hot tub, smoking a joint, and trying to convince Turner in April or May of 1984 that CNN should cover his findings about the Reagan administration secretly running guns to the Contra rebels in Central America in violation of the law and smuggling drugs back into the country. Sheehan argued that it was just the kind of story that would vault CNN into the status of a major news network.

Turner was excited about the story, jumping up and down, saying this was going to make CNN's reputation.

However, the next Monday morning, when the two of them were discussing the story with one of the CNN executives, the executive turned to Ted and said, "We can't do this story. If you try and do this story, Theodore Shackley will have you killed."

Ted immediately knew the name.

At the time Shackley was the former secret covert operations director for the CIA, handpicked years earlier by CIA Director George H. W. Bush, and rumored to still be active. Shackley was nicknamed "the blond ghost" because few people knew of his existence. He was supposedly the guy who did really bad things for the CIA, like when people needed to disappear. Sheehan wondered how this CNN executive knew of Shackley and could only conclude that the CNN executive was connected to an intelligence agency.

Shackley may have been a ghost in 1984, but by the time he died in December 2002, he'd become well known and the subject of a 1994 book titled *Blond Ghost: Ted Shackley and the CIA's Crusades*. The *New York Times* provided quite a nice obituary for the former spook:

> He served in the hot spots of West Berlin, Saigon and Vientiane, Laos, and other places in a career that lasted from 1951 to 1979. Along the way, he was involved in the spy agency's most famous and controversial undertakings.

But not as many as his biographers have written, his daughter said today. She said her father was not involved in Operation Mongoose, an intelligence operation said to have been ordered by Attorney General Robert F. Kennedy to assassinate Fidel Castro.

Nor, despite rumors to the contrary, was he involved, after leaving the CIA, in the Iran-Contra arms-for-hostages scandal that rocked the administration of President Ronald Reagan, Ms. Shackley said.

Ms. Shackley said she believed her father's assertions that he was not linked to those episodes, and believed similar statements from others in a position to know. Her father's supposed links to those affairs illustrate what happens "when fiction ultimately becomes 'fact'" through endless repetition, Ms. Shackley said.[250]

Shaheen told Turner in 1984 that he'd be "king of the world" if he published this information, but Turner couldn't get the hierarchy of CNN executives to agree. It wasn't until October 1986 that anybody covered the information Sheehan had developed, and it broke out as the Iran-Contra scandal, which nearly brought down the Reagan presidency. The only reason it got covered at the time was because the Nicaraguan government shot down a CIA plane carrying weapons shipments, and US Marine Eugene Hasenfus, the sole survivor, provided a full confession.

On the question of whether our suspicions about certain CNN personnel being connected to intelligence agencies are correct, Sheehan couldn't give a definitive answer, except to say that they were consistent with what he had seen in the past about how the intelligence agencies worked hand in glove with media outlets.

However, Sheehan recounted how he'd worked for many years with Ross Perot, first on Perot's inquiry into American soldiers left behind in Vietnam and Laos (they were usually working with the CIA's drug-smuggling operations) and then on Perot's presidential run. In a meeting with Sheehan about Perot's presidential run, a reporter for *Time* revealed that he'd been the one who spiked the story about Americans left behind in Vietnam. Sheehan could only conclude that the *Time* reporter was also an intelligence operative, so he walked out of the meeting.

Another person about whom Sheehan has long had suspicions is Bob Woodward, who early in his career was a briefer from the Office of Naval Intelligence to the Joint Chiefs of Staff. It's an extraordinarily high position for a future reporter to have. When Woodward later wanted to interview Sheehan about Perot's presidential ambitions, Sheehan declined.

From what Sheehan has learned about Project Mockingbird, it was clear that the intelligence agencies have a full-scale recruiting program to place intelligence operatives in the media for the specific purpose of shutting down stories they don't want reported. Sheehan believes this is "an infection at the very marrow of our democratic system by the national security state apparatus, the actual flow of information to people in a democracy."

Sheehan says, "Not only do they take people who are previously experienced intelligence officers and embed them in media organizations for the express purpose of killing stories they don't like, but they also try to recruit active journalists to become operatives for the CIA. They do both those things."

With all that background, Sheehan believes there's no reason that the intelligence agencies would not also try to penetrate a news organization like CNN.

For those who might argue that the revelations about Operation Mockingbird by the Church Commission in the late 1970s caused the suspension of the program, Sheehan is unconvinced. "If people don't get put in jail for something, they're going to keep doing it," he says. "Nothing happens to these people because they're perceived to be part of the national security state."

Sheehan adds, "The fact that they've infected the news media is a subset of a huge major problem of the existence of the national security state. [In another part of the interview, Sheehan also questioned whether the intelligence agencies were routinely infiltrating political organizations that might pose a threat to the established order.] It's important to write a book and maybe beat up on CNN, but this a mere subset of a very profound social policy problem we currently have."

We and our researchers couldn't find any evidence of intelligence agents being convicted of inappropriately interacting with the media or of being prosecuted for much of anything.

They exist in the shadows, and the best that the public can do is to try to peer into the darkness.

***

After the interview with Sheehan, Cary found the legal code covering how intelligence agents are allowed to work with media people and organizations. It is 50 U.S. Code, Section 3324, "Prohibition on Using Journalists as Agents or Assets," and was in effect when Cary wrote this section on March 10, 2022. Section (a) "Policy," states:

> It is the policy of the United States that an element of the Intelligence Community may not use as an agent or asset for the purposes of collecting intelligence any individual who—
>
> (1) is authorized by contract or by the issuance of press credentials to represent himself or herself, either in the United States or abroad, as a correspondent of a United States media organization; or
> (2) is officially recognized by a foreign government as a representative of a United States media organization.[251]

That would seem to settle the issue, right? There is a virtual wall between the intelligence agencies and members of the media. But then comes Section (b) "Waiver," which starts to give a little wriggle room:

> Pursuant to such procedures as the President may prescribe, the President or the Director of Central Intelligence may waive subsection (a) in the case of an individual if the President or the Director, as the case may be, makes a written determination that the waiver is necessary to address the overriding national security interest of the United States. The Permanent Select Committee on Intelligence of the House of Representatives and the Select Committee on Intelligence of the Senate shall be notified of any waiver under this subsection.[252]

One might say that seems prudent. We've got our general law, but if a situation arises that's really important, we want the president or the director of the CIA to have the freedom to take those actions necessary to protect us. Then comes section (c), which is called "Voluntary Cooperation."

> Subsection (a) shall not be construed to prohibit the voluntary cooperation of any person who is aware that the cooperation is being provided to an element of the United States Intelligence Community.[253]

Are you completely confused about what's allowed and what's prohibited? It's probably helpful to do a little role-playing to see how this might work out in the real world:

> A CIA agent approaches a member of the media and says, "Hey, I'm with the CIA, and I'd really like to work with you. But it's against the law."

The journalist, being that kind of hard-nosed, no-nonsense media type who asks the tough questions, says, "Yeah? Well, how many people have been prosecuted for violating that law?"

The CIA agent replies, "Nobody to my knowledge. But even though there will be no consequences if I violate that law, I'd still like to follow it."

"Okay," says the journalist, "is there any way we can get around that?"

"Well," replies the helpful CIA agent, "we can get the president or the director of the CIA to write a note saying it's okay. But then they'd have to give it to a special committee for both the House and Senate."

"That sounds like a lot of work," says the journalist. "Any other ideas?"

"Or," replies the CIA agent, "you could just agree to work with me."

The journalist fixes the CIA agent with a hard stare for a moment before saying, "Why didn't you just say that in the first place? Are you sure you belong to an intelligence agency? Because I'm not seeing much intelligence here."

It really is that simple for a member of the media to work with a member of an intelligence agency.

One might even be tempted to ask, "Is there even a law, if it's never enforced?"

*\*\*\**

The perspective of two experts of differing political backgrounds but with similar levels of experience with the intelligence agencies show a remarkable convergence.

The long-time FBI agent agrees with the main arguments we make, and only questions whether we have overstated the value of certain pieces of information.

The long-time constitutional lawyer believes that the information we've presented is credible, but says, if anything, we have *undervalued* the how much the intelligence agencies control various media outlets, and possibly much more.

This is not just a CNN problem, and not just a media problem, and it raises the question of how much of our national life is quietly controlled by the intelligence agencies under the guise of "national security."

# CHAPTER EIGHT

# Final Thoughts

The challenge in putting a book together such as this one is that the authors have to assemble the facts, then come to conclusions about what the facts mean. We believe that there are three possible interpretations of what we have presented.

There's a scene in the 1990 movie *The Hunt for Red October* that we always keep in mind when trying to come to a conclusion. At one point in the movie, the captain and officers of a new Soviet submarine decide to defect to the United States. They have no way to communicate this information to the Americans but hope that the right kind of person reads the clues they've left and comes to the correct conclusion.

The scene takes place near the climax of the film, as the Americans, led by CIA analyst Jack Ryan (played by Alec Baldwin), have successfully made their way onto the submarine but now find themselves under attack by another Soviet submarine. The Russian captain, Marko Ramius (played by Sean Connery in his coolest role since 007), executes a high-risk gambit to avoid the torpedo. In this moment of high tension, Captain Ramius asks Ryan about an earlier comment that he wasn't a field agent but simply wrote books for the CIA.

> Captain Ramius: What books?

> Jack Ryan: Pardon me?

> Captain Ramius: What books did you write?

> Jack Ryan: I wrote a biography about Admiral Halsey called *The Fighting Sailor* about naval combat tactics.

> Captain Ramius [Shakes his head]: I know this book. Your conclusions were all wrong, Ryan. Halsey acted stupidly.[254]

Someone can have all the information he needs, but that doesn't necessarily stop that person from coming to the wrong conclusion. We have done all we can to get our facts correct.

However, that doesn't necessarily prevent our conclusions from being wrong. Maybe all that we've presented is nothing more than a catalogue of media stupidity.

***

The second possibility comes directly from the comments of Senator Chuck Schumer in his conversation with Rachel Maddow, shortly before Trump took office.

> SENATOR CHUCK SCHUMER: Let me tell you, you take on the intelligence community, they have six ways from Sunday at getting back at you. So, even for a practical, supposedly hard-nosed businessman, he's [Trump] being really dumb to do this.[255]

Could it be so simple as Trump disrespecting the intelligence agencies and in turn they went after him "six ways from Sunday?" If so, this raises many uncomfortable questions about what we, as a country, should do with the intelligence agencies.

One month after the assassination of President John F. Kennedy in 1963, former President Harry Truman wrote a remarkable opinion piece in the *Washington Post* titled, "Limit CIA Role to Intelligence." Truman began by talking about the difficulty of knowing what was truly happening in the world:

> I wanted and needed the information in its "natural raw" state and in as comprehensive a volume as it was practical for me to make full use of it. But the most important thing about this move was to guard against the chance of intelligence being used to influence or lead the President into unwise decisions—and I thought it was necessary that the President do his own thinking.

> For some time, I have been disturbed by the way the CIA has been diverted from its original assignment. It has become an operational and at times a policy-making arm of the Government.[256]

Throughout history those who surround a leader have been suspected of manipulating that leader with false or misleading information. It's been said that the decisions one makes are only as good as the information one relies on to make those decisions. Truman was a man with a fine appreciation of these dangers.

Speaking just a month after President Kennedy's assassination, Truman knew that many people would realize that they were not getting accurate information about recent events. Was Truman calling on certain people to stand down, or was he calling for others to stand up? This is how he ended his piece:

But there are now some searching questions that need to be answered. I, therefore, would like to see the CIA be restored to its original assignment as the intelligence arm of the President, and that whatever else it can properly perform in that special field—and that its operational duties be terminated or properly used elsewhere.

We have grown up as a nation, respected for our free institutions and for our ability to maintain a free and open society. There is something about the way the CIA has been functioning that is casting a shadow over our historic position and I feel that we need to correct it.[257]

But Truman's argument did not carry the day. The CIA was not limited to intelligence gathering. Instead, the CIA continued its ways and got sixteen other brother and sister intelligence agencies, whose messages were so confusing it eventually required the creation of a "Director of National Intelligence" to make sense of the competing narratives.

Senator Schumer does not appear to share Truman's concern about the intelligence agencies and, if anything, seems to be an enthusiastic proponent of their interference in our political system.

The media, which are supposed to act as a check on power, also seemed to be going along with the playbook. In Schumer's interview with Rachel Maddow, she seemed to be terrified at the prospect of any changes in the intelligence community.

We have documented in this book many troubling connections of individuals to intelligence agencies who work at CNN, who would have been well-positioned to craft a narrative against a sitting president.

Americans must consider the possibility that a president of the United States was driven from office by the collusion of their own intelligence agencies.

***

Cary finds the third possibility the most troubling, and it came to him after reading Peter Schweizer's fine book *Red-Handed: How American Elites Get Rich Helping China Win.*[258] In the book, he details how American elites, including the Bush and Biden families, Ivy League universities, Wall Street firms, and tech giants, have been making themselves rich by helping China.

In Schweizer's view it comes down to the belief held by many among the elite that China simply has a better system, which combines state-run capitalism with state control over the political process.

What if we entertained the proposition that the intelligence agencies were not protecting American freedoms and instead had decided that Americans are not entitled to them?

It's the possibility with the least amount of evidence, but it is the best fit for what has taken place over the past several years.

It might explain some of the shenanigans in the Democratic Party as well as those on the Republican side. The genius of George Orwell's *1984* is that ruling powers realize that the people will *always* seek out a counter idea. That's why the ruling powers set up Big Brother as the government and also position Emmanuel Goldstein as the archenemy of the state.

However, there is no Goldstein. But Big Brother will track those who want to learn more about Goldstein, eventually capture them, brutalize them, and then reveal the reality that there is no Goldstein. The shattered seekers of truth return to society knowing there is no hope and, after a few years, are quietly dispatched by the state.

Does this explain why so many today see not two parties but one "establishment"?

If this scenario is correct, there is no other conclusion but that the intelligence agencies have become the enemy of the very freedoms they once sought to protect.

***

On a personal note, Cary wishes to say that his time at CNN, his whistleblowing, and working on this book have been some of the best times of his life, and some of the most challenging.

He loves his new job at Project Veritas as an investigative journalist, as well as helping prospective whistleblowers deal with the emotional toll this will take on their lives and trying to soften that blow. He is living his personal dream of being a positive force for good in the world, and it makes him happier than anything he has ever experienced.

However, the life of a whistleblower and public figure can be hard on the people around you. While Rebecca was steadfast in standing behind Cary as he underwent this ordeal, it took a toll on their marriage, and in January 2022 they made the decision to divorce. There were no issues of drug or alcohol abuse, nor infidelity. Cary and Rebecca remain in close contact, especially for the benefit of their daughter. It may sound odd to say, but they are extremely good friends, respectful and supportive of each other. Rebecca even sat for an interview for this book with Kent as she wanted to contribute her recollections, as well as express her appreciation for the Project Veritas team. Her mother, Carol, and stepfather, Tim, remain as close to Cary as family and also sat for an interview with Kent.

It is not the life that Cary wanted, but it is the life that he has, and he is making the best of it.

***

The decision to become a whistleblower against CNN was something that plagued Cary's days and made it difficult for him to sleep at night, and he often wondered if it was worth the cost.

It's true that his politics shifted over the course of his time at CNN, but that wasn't the motivation for what he did. Despite the politics, Cary believes that the media should try to get to the truth, as well as respecting the opinions of others. While Americans may argue about the issues, they must retain a sense of civility to each other.

Of all the people whom Cary recorded for Project Veritas, none was more troubling than Patrick Davis, the operations manager at CNN, who had worked for the company for twenty-five years. He seemed genuinely conflicted by what he was seeing at CNN but didn't know what to do about it. Here is part of the interview, with James O'Keefe setting up the clip, then Patrick Davis revealing his disillusionment with CNN:

> CARY POARCH: I want just the facts. The motto that CNN put out earlier this year, "Facts First," that's what I want the news to be. That's what it used to be. That's all I want to do with coming forward. I want CNN and any other outlets to return to what they once were. Where, hey, we tune in to get our facts. We can make up our minds, left, right, center, whatever. Cool. Then we go on with our lives. I don't want anyone spun into believing, or being programmed into believing, one way or the other. That's not what I'm about. And that's why I'm coming forward.

> JAMES O'KEEFE [Voiceover]: Patrick Davis, CNN's manager of field operations, has been at the network for twenty-five years. He longs for the good old days.

> PATRICK DAVIS: We could be so much better than what we are. And the buck stops with him [Zucker]. And we've had other presidents. Like, I've been through so many presidents now. Some that are so hands off that you don't even hear from them for a

month. You know what I mean? He's involved every day, has a plan, whatever. I just don't agree with it.[259]

How do you criticize a guy who's just trying to put food on the table and take care of his family? He seemed to be a genuinely good person, even if there were some issues on which we didn't agree.

Then something wonderful happened.

In the fall of 2021, James O'Keefe and Patrick Davis met at an Irish bar in Annapolis, Maryland, to talk about the state of journalism and how what Cary had filmed had changed Patrick's life. No hidden cameras. Just two people having a conversation and seeing where their discussion led them.

On February 24, 2022, O'Keefe took the stage at the annual Conservative Political Action Conference to announce that Patrick Davis, the twenty-five-year employee of CNN, winner of four Emmy Awards and three Peabody Awards, was joining Project Veritas as its executive producer. O'Keefe also presented a video that Project Veritas was releasing about the hire, along with an interview with Davis.

James sat with Patrick, who was dressed in a charcoal gray suit, blue and white shirt, and purple tie. Patrick was a new man. He was a man who was happy.

> JAMES O'KEEFE: Patrick, you've gone from CNN, field operations manager for the Washington bureau, and you have accepted a position as executive producer at Project Veritas.
>
> PATRICK DAVIS: That is correct.
>
> O'KEEFE: And people might find that interesting.
>
> DAVIS: Yeah. Look, the reality is, I was there for twenty-five years, half of my life. I gave blood, sweat, and tears to that company. I loved the people there. I still do. There are some amazing journalists who still work

there, in the office and out in the field, especially. But it got to a point where what we were doing, out in the field, and gathering news, how it was being translated on the air, wasn't what CNN was meant to be.[260]

In the video, James and Patrick talked for a few minutes about Davis's job duties at CNN, how CNN had first embraced Project Veritas when James and another undercover operative had infiltrated several ACORN offices around the country, James posing as a pimp, and a young woman posing as a prostitute, asking the organization for advice on how to best set up a brothel with underage girls. ACORN was supposed to be a voter registration and community service organization and was even supported at the time by then-Democratic presidential candidate Barack Obama.

Their conversation then shifted to the undercover video that Cary had shot. Patrick said correctly that Cary had sought him out for advice on being a mentor, both in his job and for being a husband, and it was only during the last ten minutes of their hour together that Cary shifted the conversation to CNN.

> JAMES O'KEEFE: You were called into an office, you saw this tape and you go, "Oh!" It dawned on you at that moment it was an undercover investigation, and you were an unwitting whistleblower, so to speak?

> PATRICK DAVIS: Right. Yes.

> [Tape cuts to video that Cary shot of Patrick when he was operations manager at the CNN's Washington bureau.]

> DAVIS [While operations manager]: We could be so much better than what we are.

[Tape cuts to another segment that Cary shot of Patrick at a restaurant.]

DAVIS [Operations manager): And you learn it in journalism school. We're supposed to be middle of the road. That's our job. Now, it's just infotainment, is all it's become. There is no true news media outlet.[261]

The two of them talked a little more about the situation with Jeff Zucker not wanting Patrick Davis to speak to James O'Keefe, then James segued into how Patrick's tape had provoked controversy at Project Veritas.

DAVIS: When you and I were talking on the phone that night and I was basically saying, "Dude, don't do this."

O'KEEFE: Tough call.

DAVIS: It's a tough call. It's a really difficult call.[262]

It was extremely heartwarming to watch this interaction between James O'Keefe and Patrick Davis. Cary had felt genuinely bad for secretly taping Patrick, but what he said was of public interest. However, in 2019, Cary could never have imagined that not only would there be forgiveness, but that he would actively seek to join Project Veritas.

Further on in the video, James and Patrick discussed how this remarkable change was brought about:

JAMES O'KEEFE: We met up in Annapolis in the fall of 2021. And you and I had a face-to-face conversation for, I think the first time ever.

PATRICK DAVIS: It was kind of funny how the first meeting happened. Because you and I had been kind of going back and forth a little bit. At like ten o'clock on a Friday night…

And I'm like, "You know, we should sit down and talk. It's been two years."

O'KEEFE: You and I sat down in an Irish pub in Annapolis for a few hours and talked about everything. It occurred to me in our meeting that, "Wow, this guy might make a good lead producer for Project Veritas." We both assessed each other. You came up to New York—

DAVIS: Do you know what made me decide to come to work here? It was the FBI raid [on November 6, 2021]. I thought it was the biggest abridgment to the First Amendment, maybe in the history of this country. Right? For the FBI to go blowing in the doors of journalists, it's unheard of. They were raiding your home.

O'KEEFE: You chose this place because federal agents put me in handcuffs?

DAVIS: Yeah.[263]

That exchange made Cary proud to be American. There may be things that Americans disagree on, but when it comes to their freedom, there should be no debate. We either support freedom or tyranny, and the raid on Project Veritas was the act of a tyrannical government. The conversation turned to Patrick's first few days working with Project Veritas, and his face almost seemed to glow with joy.

PATRICK DAVIS: In the first five days of working at this company I had more conversations about ethical journalism than I probably did in the last ten years of my career [at CNN]. Should we do the story? Should we not do the story? How should we go about this story? You know, this might hurt this person. And we know journalism harms people. Right? But sometimes there's a way to go about something. It just dawned on me, that it was so refreshing. It was a team of people, amazing researchers and journalists, actually work here. This is a young team, but they love journalism. They love getting to the bottom of things.[264]

The conversation continued, with James asking Patrick whether he thinks that objective journalism is possible. Patrick genuinely does, and he hopes that CNN returns to its historic roots, just as Cary had said in the 2019 Project Veritas release. James asked a final question:

JAMES O'KEEFE: What is objective journalism?

PATRICK DAVIS: It's being able to put aside your personal beliefs, and thoughts and ideas. You can bring your life experiences to the table, especially as journalists. I've never aligned myself with a party. I don't think I'll ever register with a party. And I don't think journalists should. I think our job is to try and stay as middle of the road as possible. You can vote however you want. But when you're actually involved in the story, with a candidate, or a corporation, or a drug company, or whatever it may be, you have to put that journalist hat on. And you have to set your personal politics aside.[265]

It really can't be said any better. And whether Cary supported Bernie Sanders, or somebody more conservative, he has always tried to set aside his personal beliefs and listen to what others have to say.

In 2021, Patrick and Cary met again at the Project Veritas Christmas party. Patrick told Cary that although there was no axe to bury between them; he wanted to sit and talk for a few hours. They revisited things, talked about their respective experiences, and parted with their friendship renewed.

The writing of this book has taken thousands of hours and involved many hours of Kent Heckenlively interviewing Cary, as he struggled to pull together all the various strands of this sprawling story. Recently, Kent told him, "Cary, whenever I'm working with a subject, there comes a time when I realize there's an expression the person uses which encapsulates who they are. And I've finally figured out what that expression is for you."

"What is it?" I asked.

"You love talking to people and hearing different points of view. And inevitably, there comes a time when you say to them 'fair enough,' meaning you understand what they're saying, even if you may not agree with it. But in using that expression, "fair enough," you're giving them dignity, letting them know you understand their point of view. You're letting them know you want to continue the conversation. You're telling the person that, together, we will find the answers. It's also probably part of that Southern charm thing you've got going."

Fair enough.

We hope that you will think that we've been "fair enough" as we've explored why our media has strayed so far from the basic principles. We will never be so bold as to claim that we know the truth, but we have many questions, as well as strong suspicions.

We believe that something has gone terribly wrong in our country, and in this book, we have been on the hunt for it. We hope you will join us in this mission. We feel that we've taken some shots at the beast through the dense woods, heard its howl (possibly in pain or surprise), come upon strange tracks and drops of blood on the ground, but haven't yet caught it.

We're not sure exactly what we're tracking—simple human stupidity, political bias, intelligence agencies gone rogue, or something else altogether—but we must find the beast. We must pursue this creature, corner it, and look upon its face, if we are to know which steps to take next.

We, as citizens, must not allow this beast to slip into the darkness to continue its reign of terror.

# Meet the New Boss. Same as the Old Boss?

The purpose of writing any critical book is to get those in positions of authority to consider the criticisms made and address them, either by pointing out errors in the authors' facts or conclusions, or by accepting the criticisms as valid and taking actions to correct them.

The writing of this book coincided with remarkable changes at CNN, and the eventual impact of many of these events on the company is still unclear. We did not anticipate the firing of anchor Chris Cuomo, or the resignations of CNN President, Jeff Zucker, as well as his lover and fellow executive, Allison Gollust. These events caused a significant restructuring of the book which we hope has provided a more complete picture of the network than we originally imagined we would be able to produce.

However, a deeper question remains. Are these changes of personnel merely convenient scapegoats for the mistakes made by others, or do they signal an acknowledgment of some deeper fundamental flaw in the company's philosophy, which has been a radical departure from the founding mission of Ted Turner?

Cary Poarch was first disturbed by CNN's reporting of President Trump's remarks after the Charlottesville riots in August of 2017 (the so-called "fine people hoax"), and these concerns grew as the network continued a daily assault on Trump for alleged Russian collusion, a charge definitively rejected with the release of the Mueller report on April 18, 2019. It was these concerns which led Cary to contact Project Veritas and document this anti-Trump and anti-conservative bias among CNN staff for several months.

Further investigation of CNN revealed three additional areas of concern.

First, an analysis of the social media contacts of the Biden White House suggests they favor CNN above all other news outlets, including the *New York Times* or the *Washington Post*. As any administration seeks to represent all the people, including those who did not vote for them, this narrow approach is likely to be destabilizing to vast numbers of the public who do not feel their voices are being heard.

Second, we uncovered evidence that CNN appears to be developing an exceptionally strong digital warfighting unit, raising questions about how it might seek to deploy those capacities in the future. Is it simply for the defense of CNN's digital infrastructure, or might it be used against other news agencies, or even governments?

Finally, we were surprised to discover the large number of CNN employees and on-air personnel with experience working for various branches of the intelligence agencies. The historical precedent of this is Operation Mockingbird, in which more than four hundred members of the media were revealed to have worked with the CIA, and yet due to the intervention of former CIA directors William Colby and George H.W. Bush these names were never revealed to the public, causing us to remain ignorant as to the full scope of the program. Recent efforts allowing intelligence agencies to operate in the U.S. media under the guise of fighting "disinformation" raise further suspicions as to what is taking place behind the scenes. How much, if any, of our current media is being directed by various branches of our intelligence agencies?

And yet it seems the new leadership of CNN is tackling the first issue we raised in this book: the claim of bias against political conservatives. On May 1, 2022, the new Chairman and CEO of CNN, Christopher Licht, sent a memo to CNN employees which seemed to hint at a change in direction. As reported in the *New York Post*:

> CNN's new boss kicked off his first day on the job by telling employees he wants to focus the network's reporting on news and "truth" amid criticism over the scandal-scarred network's heavy emphasis on opinion-based shows.

> Chris Licht—who officially replaced CNN's disgraced boss Jeff Zucker on Monday following stints as an executive producer at "The Late Show with Stephen Colbert" and "CBS This Morning"—circulated a memo to employees saying "too many people have lost trust in the news media."

> "I think we can be a beacon in regaining that trust by being an organization that exemplifies the best characteristics of journalism: fearlessly speaking truth to power, challenging the status quo, questioning 'group-think,' and educating viewers and readers with straightforward facts and insightful commentary, while always being respectful of differing viewpoints," Licht wrote.[266]

It was the kind of comment one imagines CNN founder Ted Turner might have made during the years he ran the network. However, not all the hosts at CNN seem to agree with the new direction Licht plans on taking the company, as this article from June of 2022 demonstrates:

> CNN primetime host Don Lemon demanded journalists not give "both sides" of the political aisle equal footing in their reporting, because Republicans are "misleading" the country while Democrats are "standing up for democracy."

> Appearing on "New Day" Wednesday morning, Lemon praised how journalism has drastically changed in the past several decades, to where he can now give his opinion while reporting because he hosts a cable news show.[267]

Is there going to be a reckoning between the views of current CNN boss, Chris Licht, and media personalities like Don Lemon? And if so, who wins that fight?

A report from Axios in June of 2022 suggests that a month into his new job, Licht is closely watching whether his hosts can handle the new direction he is asking them to take.

> CNN's new boss, Chris Licht, is evaluating whether personalities and programming that grew polarizing during the Trump era can adapt to the network's new priority to be less partisan.

> **Why it matters:** If talent cannot adjust to a less partisan tone, they could be ousted, three sources familiar with the matter tell Axios.

> **Details:** Licht wants to give personalities that may appear polarizing a chance to prove they're willing to uphold the network's values so they don't tarnish CNN's journalism brand.[268]

Despite the careful language being used by Licht, the message is clear: During the Trump years CNN was partisan in a way foreign to the traditional standards of journalism.

However, will it be so simple to steer CNN back to the calmer, less hyperkinetic world of objective journalism? The June 2022 numbers for CNN showed that the freefall of viewers since the high of January 2021 is continuing.

> CNN's primetime lineup only attracted 654,000 total viewers and 148,000 in the key advertising demographic of viewers aged 25-54—a 1-percent decline in both categories from May. And in total day viewership, CNN's overall audience dropped to 487,000 while it attracted 104,000 viewers in the 25-54 demo, shedding 3 percent and 2 percent respectively.

> And during the week of June 13 to 19, which featured quite a bit of focus on the committee hearings [January 6, 2021 Committee], the network only averaged 480,000 viewers overall, a 13-percent drop from its May averages and the channel's worst week since November 2015.[269]

In a country of more than three hundred and twenty-nine million people, CNN's primetime lineup is far below a million viewers. During this same time, the primetime lineup for Fox News was 2.17 million people, or more than three times that of CNN.[270] Even when the 1.28 million nightly viewers for MSNBC[271] are added to the mix that means only a little over four million people, slightly more than one percent of the population, are watching the main cable news channels.

We believe it will be much more difficult than the executives at CNN believe, because their most recent pronouncements hint at a confession that they have grossly violated the trust of their audience.

Telling your news reporters they need to be objective is like a wife reminding her husband not to sleep with other women. It's simply one of those expectations we don't feel the need to put into words because everybody understands the concept. When trust is violated at such a deep level it is difficult, if not impossible, to regain the original level of trust. Imagine a husband who says to his wife, "I've been cheating on you for ten years, but the good news is I've stopped now!" How many wives would be willing to wait around to see if the claim is true? And even if the intention to not cheat in the future was genuine, how many could forgive the years of betrayal?

This book has been primarily about CNN, but we suspect the problems we have highlighted to be common throughout the media landscape, including Fox News, MSNBC, and others. The public is aware of how the press is supposed to act and has been witness to many violations of that fundamental expectation of fairness.

Can media organizations like CNN do the hard work of looking deeply at what they have done and reforming themselves? And even if in the future CNN acted in perfect accordance with traditional standards of journalistic objectivity, would their viewers ever return in their zenith numbers and continue to follow the network? The viewers might respond by saying, "You lied to me before about the news. How do I know you're not lying now?"

In the final analysis, the new owners of CNN might find it a better financial decision to simply dissolve the news network and start over. Perhaps a modern-day Ted Turner will arise from the rubble of our current media environment and create a news network which remains forever faithful to the ideals of a free and fair press.

That would be a victory for all Americans, right, left, and center, and an enduring legacy for the generations of journalists who have struggled, often against great odds, to bring us the truth.

# NOTES

1   "CNN's First Broadcast, June 1, 1980," YouTube video 1:41, June 1, 2011, www.youtube.com/watch?v=dqDopY5dMD8&t=3s.

2   Dan Schlossberg, "These Five Legendary Club Owners Belong in the Baseball Hall of Fame," *Forbes*, December 23, 2021, https://www.forbes.com/sites/danschlossberg/2021/12/23/these-five-legendary-club-owners-belong-in-the-baseball-hall-of-fame/?sh=27fd0116ca05.

3   Priscilla Painton, "The Taming of Ted Turner," *Time*, January 6, 1992, http://content.time.com/time/subscriber/article/0,33009,974622-6,00.html.

4   Ibid.

5   Ibid.

6   Ibid.

7   Ibid.

8   Jon Rawl, "Ted Turner: Mouth of the South," *Y'all: The Magazine of Southern People* (Winter 2009), www.tedturner.com/2009/12/ted-turnermouth-of-the-south/.

9   "Ted Turner Is Time Magazine Man of the Year," *Los Angeles Times*, December 29, 1991, www.latimes.com/archives/la-xpm-1991-12-29-mn-2116-story.html.

10  Painton, "Taming of Ted Turner."

11  "Turner Ranches FAQ," Turner Enterprises, January 18, 2022, www.tedturner.com/turner-ranches/turner-ranches-faq/.

12  Painton, "Taming of Ted Turner."

13  David Kohn, "The Mouth from the South," *60 Minutes*, February 5, 2003, www.cbsnews.com/news/the-mouth-from-the-south/?intcid=CNI-00-10aaa3b.

14  Lisa Napoli, "How Ted Turner's Vision for CNN Sparked the 24-Hour News Cycle," *Here and Now*, WBUR Boston, May 12, 2020, www.wbur.org/hereandnow/2020/05/12/cnn-ted-turner-lisa-napoli.

15  Ibid.

16  Eugene Kiely and Robert Farley, "Trump Press Conference, in Context," FactCheck.org, August 16, 2017, www.factcheck.org/2017/08/trump-press- conference-context/.

17  "Remarks on Signing the VA Choice and Quality Employment Act of 2017 in Bedminster, New Jersey, August 12, 2017," The American Presidency Project—UC Santa Barbara, October 30, 2021, www.presidency.ucsb.edu/documents/remarks-signing-the-va-choice-and-quality-employment-act-2017-bedminster-new-jersey.

18  "Man Who Saved Fiancée Would Do It Again," New Day, CNN, August 13, 2017, www.cnn.com/videos/us/2017/08/15/man-saves-fiance-intv-charlottesville-attack.cnn.

19  Jessica Estepa, "Read President Trump's Full Statement on Charlottesville Violence," USA Today, August 14, 2017, www.usatoday.com/story/news/politics/onpolitics/2017/08/14/transcript-donald-trump-remarks-charlottesville-violence/565330001/.

20  "Full Transcript and Video: Trump's News Conference in New York," New York Times, August 15, 2017, www.nytimes.com/2017/08/15/us/politics/trump-press-conference-transcript.html.

21  Nicole Chavez, Emanuella Grinberg, and Eliot C. McLaughlin, "Pittsburgh Synagogue Gunman Said He Wanted All Jews to Die, Criminal Complaint Says," CNN, October 31, 2018, www.cnn.com/2018/10/28/us/pittsburgh-synagogue-shooting/index.html.

22  Ibid.

23  Alex Ward, "Trump Calls the Pittsburgh Shooting 'Anti-Semitic' and a 'Wicked Act of Mass Murder,'" Vox, October 27, 2018, www.vox.com/2018/10/27/18032692/trump-pittsburgh-shooting-synagogue-semitism-murder.

24  Ibid.

25  James O'Keefe, "They Can Stop One of Us, but They Can't Stop an Army," CPAC 2019, YouTube, March 2, 2019 (transcription by Kent Heckenlively), www.youtube.com/watch?v=ciOU_KSh6PY.

26  "Part 1: CNN Insider Blows Whistle on Network President Jeff Zucker's Personal Vendetta Against POTUS," Project Veritas, October 14, 2019, www.youtube.com/watch?v=m7XZmugtLv4.

27  Ibid.

28  "CNN Field Manager: Zucker's 9 a.m. Calls 'B.S.'…Totally Left Leaning… Don't Want to Admit It," Project Veritas, October 17, 2019, https://www.youtube.com/watch?v=qbQwAQ0tDTQ.

29  Ibid.

30  Ibid.

31  Jeffrey Toobin, "An Incendiary Defense," New Yorker, July 18, 1994, www.newyorker.com/1994/07/25/an-incendiary-defense.

32  Laura Wagner, "*New Yorker* Suspends Jeffrey Toobin for Masturbating on Zoom Call," *Vice*, October 19, 2020, www.vice.com/en/article/epdgm4/new-yorker-suspends-jeffrey-toobin-for-zoom-dick-incident.

33  Kate Sheehy, "Accused Zoom Masturbator Jeffrey Toobin Has Naughty Sex History," *New York Post*, October 20, 2020, www.nypost.com/2020/10/20/accused-zoom-masturbator-jeffrey-toobin-has-sordid-sex-history/.

34  Gabrielle Fonrouge, "Jeffrey Toobin Partied with CNN Colleagues after Return from Masturbation Scandal," *New York Post*, June 16, 2021, www.nypost.com/2021/06/16/jeffrey-toobin-partied-with-cnn-anchors-execs-after-return/.

35  Brian Flood, "CNN Gives Jeffrey Toobin Front-Row Seat for Announcement of Chris Cuomo's Suspension, Conjuring Up Comparisons," Fox News, December1,2021,www.foxnews.com/media/cnn-toobin-front-row-announcement-cuomos-suspension.

36  "Report of Investigation into Allegations of Sexual Harassment by Governor Andrew M. Cuomo," State of New York, Office of the Attorney General, August 3, 2021, p. 1, www.ag.ny.gov/sites/default/files/2021.08.03_nyag_-_investigative_report.pdf.

37  Ibid., 1, f2.

38  Ibid., 24–25.

39  Ibid., 35.

40  Ibid., 36.

41  Ibid., 38.

42  Ibid., 99–100.

43  Ibid., 100.

44  Ibid., 164.

45  "Additional Transcripts, Exhibits, and Videos from Independent Investigation into Sexual Harassment Allegations against Former Governor Cuomo Released—Chris Cuomo Exhibits," State of New York, Office of the Attorney General, June 28, 2021, p. 159, www.ag.ny.gov/sites/default/files/chris_cuomo_exhibits_-_combined.pdf.

46  Ibid., 160.

47  Ibid., 161.

48  Froma Harrop, "Women Accusing Cuomo Won't Come Out on Top," *Newsweek*, March 4, 2021, www.newsweek.com/women-accusing-cuomo-wont-come-out-top-opinion-1573595.

49  "Additional Transcripts, Exhibits, and Videos From Independent Investigation into Sexual Harassment Allegations Against Former Governor Cuomo Released – Chris Cuomo Exhibits" Office of New York State Attorney General, Leticia James, November 29, p. 163, www.ag.ny.gov/sites/default/files/chris_cuomo_exhibits_-_combined.pdf.

50  Ibid., 165.

51  Michael M. Grynbaum, John Koblin, and Jodi Kantor, "CNN Fires Chris Cuomo amid Inquiry into His Brother's Efforts to Aid His Brother," *New York Times*, December 4, 2021, www.nytimes.com/2021/12/04/business/media/chris-cuomo-fired-cnn.html.

52  Christina Maxouris, "CNN Producer John Griffin Arrested for Attempting to Persuade Minors to Engage in Unlawful Sexual Activity," CNN, December 11, 2021, www.cnn.com/2021/12/11/us/john-griffin-charged-arrested-minors-unlawful-sexual-activity/index.html.

53  "Connecticut Man Indicted for Attempting to Induce Minors to Engage in Unlawful Sexual Activity at Ludlow Residence," United States Attorney's Office, District of Vermont, press release, December 10, 2021, www.justice.gov/usao-vt/pr/connecticut-man-indicted-attempting-induce-minors-engage-unlawful-sexual-activity-ludlow.

54  Jordan Dixon-Hammer, "Fairfax County Police: Former Jake Tapper Producer Under Investigation by Child Exploitation Squad," Breitbart, December 28, 2021, www.breitbart.com/the-media/2021/12/28/fairfax-county-police-confirm-jake-tapper-producer-investigated-child-exploitation-squad/.

55  "Project Veritas Names CNN Producer Involved in Wednesday's Tragic Story," Project Veritas, December 17, 2021, www.projectveritas.com/news/project-veritas-names-cnn-producer-involved-in-wednesdays-tragic-story/.

56  Brian Stelter and Oliver Darcy, "CNN President Jeff Zucker Resigns Over Consensual Relationship with Key Lieutenant," CNN, February 2, 2022.

57  Ibid.

58  Ariel Zilber, "Katie Couric Flagged Jeff Zucker's 'Super Strange' Ties to Allison Gollust in Her Memoir," *New York Post*, February 2, 2002, https://nypost.com/2022/02/02/katie-couric-flagged-jeff-zuckers-super-strange-ties-with-allison-gollust-in-memoir/.

59  Stelter and Darcy, "CNN President Jeff Zucker Resigns."

60  Ibid.

61  Pam Key, "CNN's Camerota on Zucker Exit: 'Feels Wrong' Two Consenting Adults Can't Have a Private Relationship," Breitbart, February 2, 2022, https://www.breitbart.com/clips/2022/02/02/cnns-camerota-on-zucker-exit-feels-wrong-two-consenting-adults-cant-have-a-private-relationship/.

62  Ibid.

63  Benjamin Mullin, "Chris Cuomo's Legal Team Raised Questions to CNN about Jeff Zucker's Relationship," *Wall Street Journal*, February 3, 2022, www.wsj.com/articles/chris-cuomos-legal-team-raised-questions-to-cnn-about-jeff-zuckers-relationship-11643940802.

64  Ibid.

65  Emily Smith and Theo Wayt, "Zucker, Gollust's Cozy Ties with Andrew Cuomo Included Coaching Him on COVID Briefings," *New York Post*,

February 3, 2022, www.nypost.com/2022/02/03/jeff-zucker-allison-gollusts-cozy-ties-with-andrew-cuomo-deeper-than-previously-known/.

66 Cortney O'Brien, "Brian Stelter Calls Zucker Exit 'Ugliest Shakeup' in Years, Traces Downfall to Cuomos: 'Almost Shakespearean,'" Fox News, February 6, 2022, www.foxnews.com/media/brian-stelter-zucker-exit-ugliest-shakeup-years-downfall-cuomos-almost-shakespearean.

67 Brian Stelter, "CNN Fires Chris Cuomo," CNN, December 5, 2021, www.cnn.com/2021/12/04/media/cnn-fires-chris-cuomo/index.html.

68 Brian Flood, "Bromance Over? Don Lemon Slams Former CNN Bestie Chris Cuomo for Breaking 'Journalistic Standards,'" Fox News, February 8, 2022, www.foxnews.com/media/bromance-over-don-lemon-chris-cuomo-cnn.

69 *Post* Editorial Board, "Jeff Zucker's Real Crime? Helping Andrew Cuomo," *New York Post*, February 3, 2022, www.nypost.com/2022/02/03/jeff-zuckers-real-crime-helping-andrew-cuomo/.

70 Ibid.

71 Justin Baragona, "CNN Bottomed Out in 2021—Will Viewers Come Back?" *The Daily Beast*, December 24, 2021, www.thedailybeast.com/cnn-bottomed-out-in-2021-will-viewers-come-back.

72 Brian Stelter, "Top CNN Exec Resigns as WarnerMedia Chief Accuses Her and Former Network Boss Zucker of Standards Violations," CNN, February 20, 2022, www.cnn.com/2022/02/15/media/jeff-zucker-allison-gollust/index.html.

73 Ibid.

74 Matthew J. Belvedere, "John Malone Says WarnerMedia-Discovery Getting Rid of CNN Would Be the Coward's Way Out," CNBC, November 18, 2021, https://www.cnbc.com/2021/11/18/john-malone-says-warnermedia-discovery-getting-rid-of-cnn-would-be-the-cowards-way-out.html.

75 Ibid.

76 Benjamin Mullin, "CNN Employees Grill WarnerMedia CEO Over Jeff Zucker's Departure," *Wall Street Journal*, February 2, 2022, www.wsj.com/articles/cnn-employees-grill-warnermedia-ceo-over-jeff-zuckers-departure-11643863540.

77 Ibid.

78 "Part 1: CNN Director ADMITS Network Engaged in 'Propaganda' to Remove Trump from Presidency," Project Veritas, April 13, 2021, YouTube video, www.youtube.com/watch?v=Dv8Zy-JwXr4.

79 Ibid.

80 Ibid.

81 Ibid.

82 "Part 2: CNN Director Reveals That Network Practices 'Art of Manipulation' to 'Change the World,'" Project Veritas, April 14, 2021, YouTube video, https://www.youtube.com/watch?v=9faQkIA6YNU.

83 Ibid.

[84] Ibid.

[85] "Part 3: Chester Says CNN 'Trying to Help' Black Lives Matter by Protecting Group's Narrative on Race," Project Veritas, April 15, 2021, YouTube, www.youtube.com/watch?v=R7mdc1r5-vw.

[86] Ibid.

[87] Chris Cillizza, "Anthony Fauci Just Crushed Donald Trump's Theory on the Origins of the Coronavirus," CNN, May 5, 2020, www.cnn.com/2020/05/05/politics/fauci-trump-coronavirus-wuhan-lab/index.html.

[88] Ibid.

[89] "Military Documents about Gain of Function Contradict Fauci Testimony Under Oath," Project Veritas, January 10, 2022, www.projectveritas.com/news/military-documents-about-gain-of-function-contradict-fauci-testimony-under/.

[90] Ibid.; DARPA, "Broad Agency Announcement, PREventing EMerging Pathogenic Threats (PREEMPT), Biological Technologies Office, HR001118S0017, January 19, 2018, www.assets.ctfassets.net/syq3snmxclc9/6K3RxB1DVf6ZhVxQLSJzxl/6be5c276bc8af7921ce6b23f0975a6c3/A_prempt-background-hr001118s0017.pdf.

[91] "Military Documents about Gain of Function Contradict Fauci Testimony Under Oath"; Dr. Peter Daszak, "Executive Summary: DEFUSE," EcoHealth Alliance, https://assets.ctfassets.net/syq3snmxclc9/4NFC6M83ewzKLf6DvAygb4/0cf477f75646e718afb332b7ac6c3cd1/defuse-proposal_watermark_Redacted.pdf

[92] Ibid.

[93] Ibid.

[94] "Military Documents about Gain of Function Contradict Fauci Testimony Under Oath"; https://assets.ctfassets.net/syq3snmxclc9/4NFC6M83ewzKLf6DvAygb4/0cf477f75646e718afb332b7ac6c3cd1/defuse-proposal_watermark_ Redacted.pdf

[95] Ibid.

[96] Ibid.

[97] Nick Turse, "DARPA's Wild Kingdom," *Mother Jones*, March 8, 2004, www.motherjones.com/politics/2004/03/darpas-wild-kingdom.

[98] Charles Pillar, "Army of Extreme Thinkers," *Los Angeles Times*, August 14, 2003.

[99] Turse, "DARPA's Wild Kingdom."

[100] Ibid.

[101] Ibid.

[102] Ibid.

[103] "Military Documents about Gain of Function Contradict Fauci Testimony Under Oath," *Project Veritas*, January 10, 2022, www.projectveritas.com/news/military-documents-about-gain-of-function-contradict-fauci-testimony-under/, www.assets.ctfassets.net/

syq3snmxclc9/5OjsrkkXHfuHps6
Lek1MO0/5e7a0d86d5d67e8d153555400d9dcd17/defuse-project-rejection-by-darpa.pdf.

[104] "Rejection of Defuse Project Proposal," https://drasticresearch.files.
wordpress.com/2021/09/defuse-project-rejection-by-darpa.pdf.

[105] Ibid.

[106] Glenn Owen, "REVEALED: U.S. Government Gave $3.7 Million Grant to
Wuhan Lab at Center of Coronavirus Leak Scrutiny That Was Performing
Experiments on Bats from Caves Where the Disease Is Believed to Have
Originated," *Daily Mail*, April 11, 2020, www.dailymail.co.uk/news/article-
8211291/U-S-government-gave-3-7million-grant-Wuhan-lab-
experimented-coronavirus-source-bats.html.

[107] Andrew Mark Miller, "Fox News Special Report Outlines Fresh Questions
on What Fauci, Government Knew about COVID Origin," Fox News,
January 25, 2022, www.foxnews.com/politics/special-report-outlines-fresh-
questions-on-what-fauci-government-knew-about-covid-origin.

[108] Ibid.

[109] Andrew White, "REPORT: Peter Daszak Worked for CIA, EcoHealth
Alliance Is a 'CIA Front Organization,'" *National File*, January 20, 2022,
www.nationalfile.com/report-peter-daszak-worked-cia-ecohealth-alliance-
cia-front-organization/.

[110] Ibid.

[111] Rebecca Robbins, "Drug Makers Now Spend $5 Billion a Year on
Advertising. Here's What That Buys," STAT, March 9, 2016, www.statnews.
com/2016/03/09/drug-industry-advertising/

[112] Ibid.

[113] Beth Snyder Bulik, "The Top 10 Ad Sepnders in Big Pharma for 2020," Fierce
Pharma, April 19, 2021, www.fiercepharma.com/special-report/top-10-ad-
spenders-big-pharma-for-2020.

[114] Benjamin Franklin, writing as Silence Dogood, "Eighth Letter to the Editor,"
*New England Courant,* July 9, 1722, www.founders.archives.gov/documents/
Franklin/01-01-02-0015.

[115] First Amendment to the United States Constitution, December 15, 1791,
Constitution Annotated, www.constitution.congress.gov/constitution/
amendment-1/#:~:text=Congress%20shall%20make%20no%20law,for%20
a%20redress%20of%20grievances.

[116] Byron R. White, Harry A. Blackmun, Hugo L. Black, Per Curiam, Thurgood
Marshall and Warren E. Burger, "New York Times Co. v. United States,"
edited by Joseph R. Fornieri, Teaching American History, June 30, 1971,
www.teachingamericanhistory.org/document/new-york-times-co-v-
united-states/.

[117] Daniel Strauss, "Why Symone Sanders Went from Bernie to Biden," *Politico*, December 22, 2019, www.politico.com/news/magazine/2019/12/22/symone-sanders-bernie-to-biden-088264.

[118] Ankur Kalra and Kelly Davis, "Accelerating ML within CNN," https://medium.com/cnn-digital/accelerating-ml-within-cnn-983f6b7bd2eb.

[119] Ibid.

[120] "Work We've Done," Hop Labs, February 25, 2022, www.hoplabs.com/work.

[121] Nicole Martin, "Did a Robot Write This? How AI Is Impacting Journalism," *Forbes*, February 8, 2019, www.forbes.com/sites/nicolemartin1/2019/02/08/did-a-robot-write-this-how-ai-is-impacting-journalism/.

[122] David D. Kirkpatrick, "Who Is Behind QAnon? Linguistic Detectives Find Fingerprints," *New York Times*, February 19, 2022, www.nytimes.com/2022/02/19/technology/qanon-messages-authors.html.

[123] Ibid.

[124] Ibid.

[125] Deepna Devkar, LinkedIn, February 26, 2022, www.linkedin.com/in/deepnadevkar/.

[126] Krystal Paden, LinkedIn, February 26, 2022, www.linkedin.com/in/krystal-paden-mba-a6717233/.

[127] Bo Williams, LinkedIn, February 26, 2022, www.linkedin.com/in/bowilliams/.

[128] Miguel Perez, LinkedIn, February 26, 2022, www.linkedin.com/in/mperezuncrutugers/.

[129] Ashok Chandrashekar, LinkedIn, February 26, 2022, www.linkedin/com/in/ashok-chandrashekar-31195154.

[130] Kelly Davis, LinkedIn, February 26, 2022, www.linkedin.com/in/kldavis4/.

[131] Haile Owusu, LinkedIn, February 26, 2022, www.linkedin.com/in/haileowusu.

[132] Edwin Covert, LinkedIn, February 26, 2022, www.linkedin.com/ecovert/.

[133] "Jeff Yang, Research Director," Rand Corporation, Institute for the Future (accessed February 26, 2022), www.iftf.org/jeffyang/.

[134] "Wargaming," Rand Corporation, February 26, 2022, www.rand.org/topics/wargaming.html.

[135] Diede de Kok, LinkedIn, February 26, 2022, www.uk.linkedin.com/in/diede-de-kok-0b95b158/en.

[136] Ibid.

[137] Joe Concha, "Carl Bernstein: Situation with Trump Is 'Worse than Watergate,'" *The Hill*, August 3, 2018, https://thehill.com/homenews/media/400295-carl-bernstein-situation-with-trump-is-worse-than-watergate/.

[138] Alexis Benveniste, "Carl Bernstein: Trump Is a 'War Criminal,'" CNN, July 25, 2021, www.cnn.com/2021/07/25/business/bernstein-trump-reliable/index.html.

[139] Joseph A. Wulfsohn, "Carl Bernstein Mocked for Claiming Every Trump Controversy Is 'Worse than Watergate,'" Fox News, January 4, 2021, https://www.foxnews.com/media/carl-bernstein-mocked-for-claiming-every-trump-controversy-is-worse-than-watergate.

[140] Carl Bernstein, "The CIA and the Media," *Rolling Stone*, October 20, 1977, https://www.carlbernstein.com/the-cia-and-the-media-rolling-stone-10-20-1977.

[141] Ibid.

[142] Ibid.

[143] Ibid.

[144] Ibid.

[145] Ibid.

[146] Ibid.

[147] Melissa Dykes, "Flashback: We'll Know Our Disinformation Campaign Is Successful When Everything the American Public Believes Is False," Truth Stream Media, January 13, 2015, https://truthstreammedia.com/2015/01/13/cia-flashback-well-know-our-disinformation-program-is-complete-when-everything-the-american-public-believes-is-false/.

[148] Jack Anderson, "CIA's Misleading Tactics," *Santa Cruz Sentinel*, September 22, 1981.

[149] Bob Woodward, *Veil: The Secret Wars of the CIA, 1981–1987* (New York: Simon & Schuster, 1987), 516.

[150] Ibid.

[151] Ibid.

[152] President Barack Obama, "Executive Order 13721: Developing an Integrated Global Engagement Center to Support Government-wide Counterterrorism Communications and Revoking Executive Order 13584," *Federal Register*, March 14, 2016, www.federalregister.gov/documents/2016/03/17/2016-06250/developing-an-integrated-global-engagement-center-to-support-government-wide-counterterrorism.

[153] Ibid.

[154] "Global Engagement Center, Core Mission and Vision," US Department of State (accessed February 8, 2022), www.state.gov/bureaus-offices/under-secretary-for-public-diplomacy-and-public-affairs/global-engagement-center/.

[155] US Senator Rob Portman (R-OH), "President Signs Portman-Murphy Counter-Propaganda Bill into Law," press release, December 23, 2016, https://www.portman.senate.gov/newsroom/press-releases/president-signs- portman-murphy-counter-propaganda-bill-law.

[156] *The Rachel Maddow Show*, MSNBC, January 3, 2017, www.msnbc.com/transcripts/rachel-maddow-show/2017-01-03-msna973326.

[157] "CCN Profiles: Bianca Nobilo, CNN Anchor and Correspondent," CNN, February 7, 2022, www.cnn.com/profiles/bianca-nobilo#about.

158 Ibid.
159 Ibid.
160 Bianca Nobilo, LinkedIn, February 8, 2022), www.linkedin.com/in/biancanobilo-bb7934209/.
161 "CNN Profiles: Bob Ortega, Senior Writer, CNN Investigates," CNN, February 8, 2022, www.cnn.com/profiles/bob-ortega.
162 Ibid.
163 Bob Ortega, LinkedIn, February 8, 2022, www.linkedin.com/in/bob- ortega-b998492a.
164 "CNN Profiles: Jim Sciutto, Anchor and National Security Correspondent," CNN, February 10, 2022, www.cnn.com/profiles/jim-sciutto.
165 Ibid.
166 Jim Sciutto, LinkedIn, February 10, 2022, www.linkedin.com/in/jim-sciutto-62a274/.
167 Ibid.
168 Josh Campbell, LinkedIn, February 10, 2022, www.linkedin.com/in/jim-sciutto-62a274/.
169 "CNN Profiles: Josh Campbell, Correspondent," CNN, February 10, 2022, www.cnn.com/profiles/josh-campbell.
170 Josh Campbell, LinkedIn.
171 "CNN Profiles: Josh Campbell."
172 Nicholas Best, LinkedIn, February 10, 2022, www.linkedin.com/in/nckbst.
173 Ibid.
174 Ibid.
175 Kimberly Dozier, LinkedIn, February 10, 2022, www.linkedin.com/in/kimberlydozier.
176 Ibid.
177 "Kimberly Dozier: Journalist/Broadcaster/Author," Kimberly Dozier personal website, February 10, 2022, www.kimberlydozier.com/bio/.
178 Kimberly Dozier, LinkedIn.
179 Ibid.
180 Juliette Kayyem, LinkedIn, February 10, 2022, www.linkedin.com/in/juliettekayyem/.
181 Ibid.
182 "About Me," Juliette Kayyem personal website, February 10, 2022, www.juliettekayyem.com/about/.
183 Juliette Kayyem, LinkedIn.
184 Lindsay Kornick, "CNN Analyst Calls to 'Slash the Tires' of the Canadian Trucker Convoy," Fox News, February 10, 2022, www.foxnews.com/media/cnn-analyst-slash-the-tires-canadian-trucker-convoy.
185 Ibid.
186 Melanie Lawrence, LinkedIn, February 10, 2022, www.linkedin.com/in/melanielawrence1/.

187 "NIU History," National Intelligence University, February 10, 2022, www.ni-u.edu/wp/about-niu/niu-history/.

188 Ibid.

189 Melanie Lawrence, LinkedIn.

190 "Psychometrist," Explore Health Careers, February 10, 2020, www.explorehealthcareers.org/career/mental-health/psychometrist.

191 Melanie Lawrence, LinkedIn.

192 "About Cedric Leighton," Cedric Leighton Associates, February 10, 2022, www.cedricleighton.com/about/.

193 Cedric Leighton, LinkedIn, February 11, 2022, www.linkedin.com/cedricleighton/.

194 Ibid.

195 Amber Benjamin, LinkedIn, February 11, 2022, www.linkedin.com/in/abenjamin2/.

196 Ibid.

197 Andre Lawrence, LinkedIn, February 11, 2022, www.linkedin.com/inandrelawrence/.

198 Ibid.

199 Ibid.

200 Andrew McCabe, LinkedIn, February 11, 2022, www.linked.com/in/andrew-mccabe-422664213/.

201 Ibid.

202 Ibid.

203 Matt Zapotsky, "Inspector General Report Faults Andrew McCabe for Unauthorized Disclosure of Information, Misleading Investigators," April 13, 2018, *Washington Post*, www.washingtonpost.com/world/national-security/justice-department-inspector-general-provides-report-to-congress-on-andrew-mccabe/2018/04/13/ce367c4c-3f36-11e8-974f-aacd97698cef_story.html.

204 Ibid.

205 Arnaud Siad, LinkedIn, February 11, 2022, www.linked.com/in/arnaudsiad.

206 Ibid.

207 Pete Licata, LinkedIn, February 11, 2022, www.linkedin.com/in/peterflicata.

208 Ibid.

209 Ibid.

210 Ibid.

211 Ibid.

212 Jamie Gangel, LinkedIn, February 11, 2022, www.linkedin.com/in/jamie-gangel-b65557a9/.

213 Marie Brenner, "'I Had No Problem Being Politically Different,' Young William Barr among the Manhattan Liberals," *Vanity Fair*, October 7, 2019, www.vanityfair.com/news/2019/10/the-untold-tale-of-young-william-barr.

214 Ibid.

215 Ibid.

216 "Meet William Barr, The (CIA) Man You Never Got to Know," Governmental Services Watch Corporation, October 25, 2020, www. govbanknotes.wordpress.com/2020/10/25/meet-william-barr-the-man-you-never-got-to-know/.

217 Calvin Sims, LinkedIn, February 12, 2022, www.linkedin.com/in/clavin-sims-7918034/.

218 Ibid.

219 Ibid.

220 "CNN Profiles: Fareed Zakaria, Host," CNN, February 11, 2022, www.cnn.com/profiles/fareed-zakaria-profile.

221 Ibid.

222 Fareed Zakaria, LinkedIn, February 11, 2022, www.linked-in.com/in/fareedzakaria/.

223 "Anthony J. Ferrante, Senior Managing Director, Global Head of Cybersecurity," FTI Consulting, February 13, 2022, https://www.fticonsulting.com/experts/anthony-j-ferrante.

224 Anthony J. Ferrante, LinkedIn, February 13, 2022, www.linkedin.com/in/anthony/jferrante/details/experience/.

225 Shawn Turner, LinkedIn, February 13, 2022, www.linkedin.com/in/shawn-turner-22aa0418/details/experience/.

226 Ibid.

227 Ibid.

228 Ibid.

229 Ibid.

230 Ibid.

231 "Shawn Turner: Former Terker Distinguished Fellow," George Washington School of Media and Public Affairs, February 13, 2022, www.smpa.gwu.edu/turner-shawn.

232 Rodney Hirsch, LinkedIn, February 13, 2022, www.linkedin.com/in/rodeny-hirsch-cpp/details/experience/.

233 Ibid.

234 Ibid.

235 Bethany Crudele Jones, LinkedIn, February 14, 2022, www.linkedin.com/in/bethany-crudele-jones-cnn/details/experience/.

236 Ibid.

237 Ibid.

238 Ibid.

239 Ibid.

240 Jack Shafer, "The Spies Who Came into the TV Studio," *Politico*, February 6, 2018, www.politico.com/magazine/story/2018/02/06/john-brennan-james-claper-michael-hayden-former-cia-media-216943/.

241 Ibid.

242 Ibid.

243 Ibid.

244 Telephone interview by Kent Heckenlively with FBI Agent X, March 7, 2022.

245 Thomas J. Baker, "What Are the FBI and CIA Hiding?" *Wall Street Journal*, July 31, 2018, www.wsj.com/articles/what-are-the-fbi-and-cia-hiding-1533078662.

246 Ibid.

247 Ibid.

248 Thomas J. Baker, "How to Restore the FBI's Culture," *Wall Street Journal*, August 27, 2018, www.wsj.com/articles/how-to-restore-the-fbis-culture-1535408984.

249 Telephone interview by Kent Heckenlively with Daniel Sheehan, March 9, 2022.

250 David Stout, "Theodore Shackley, Enigmatic C.I.A. Official, Dies at 75," *New York Times*, December 14, 2002, https://www.nytimes.com/2002/12/14/us/theodore-shackley-enigmatic-cia-official-dies-at-75.html.

251 "50 USC, Section 3324, Prohibition on Using Journalists as Assets," Government Regulations, March 10, 2022, www.govregs.com/uscode/title50_chapter45_subchapterII_section3324.

252 Ibid.

253 Ibid.

254 *The Hunt for Red October*, directed by John McTiernan (Hollywood: Paramount Pictures, 1990).

255 *The Rachel Maddow Show*, MSNBC, January 3, 2017, www.msnbc.com/transcripts/rachel-maddow-show/2017-01-03-msna973326.

256 Harry S. Truman, "Limit CIA Role to Intelligence," *Washington Post*, December 22, 1963, https://ia801309.us.archive.org/20/items/LimitCIARoleToIntelligenceByHarry TrumanarrySTruman/Limit%20CIA%20Role%20To%20Intelligence%20by%20Harry%20S%20Truman.pdf.

257 Ibid.

258 Peter Schweizer, *Red-Handed: How American Elites Get Rich Helping China Win* (New York: Harper, January 25, 2022).

259 "CNN Field Manager: Zucker's 9 a.m. Calls 'B.S.'…Totally Left Leaning…Don't Want to Admit It," Project Veritas, October 17, 2019, https://www.youtube.com/watch?v=qbQwAQ0tDTQ.

260 "Twenty-Five Year CNN Operations Manager Joins Project Veritas as Executive Producer," Project Veritas, February 24, 2022, https://www.projectveritas.com/news/twenty-five-year-cnn-operations-manager-joins-project-veritas-as-executive/.

261 Ibid.

262 Ibid.

263 Ibid.

264 Ibid.

265 Ibid.

266 Alexandra Steingrad, "New CNN Boss Chris Licht to Focus on 'Truth' after Slew of Scandals," May 2, 2022, *New York Post*, www.nypost. com/2022/05/02/new-cnn-boss-chris-licht-to-focus-on-truth/.

267 Kristine Parks, "CNN's Don Lemon Tells Fellow Journalists: No 'False Sense of Equivalency' Between Republicans, Democrats," June 15, 2022, *Fox News*, www.foxnews.com/media/cnns-don-lemon-tells-journalists-false-equivalency-republicans-democrats.

268 Sara Fischer, "Scoop: CNN Evaluating Partisan Talent," June 7, 2022, Axios, www.axios.com/2022/06/07/cnn-evaluating-partisan-talent-chris-licht.

269 Justin Baragona, "Not Even a New Boss Can Stop CNN's Ratings Freefall," July 1, 2022, *The Daily Beast*, www.thedailybeast.com/even-a-new-boss-cant-stop-cnns-ratings-freefall.

270 A.J. Katz, "June 2022 Cable Network Ranker: Fox News Remains Most Watched in Total Day and Prime; MSNBC's Rating Growth Driven by Jan. 6 Hearings," June 29, 2022, *Ad Week*, www.adweek.com/tvnewser/june-2022-cable-network-ranker-fox-news-remains-most-watched-in-total-day-and-prime-msnbcs-ratings-growth-driven-by-jan-6-hearings/510124/.

271 Ibid.

# ACKNOWLEDGMENTS

## Kent Heckenlively

I'd first like to thank my wonderful partner in life, Linda, and our two children, Jacqueline and Ben for their constant love and support. You make this life worthwhile. I'd also like to thank my mother, Josephine, and my father, Jack, for teaching me to have courage for the fight and respect for others. I have the best brother in the world, Jay, and am appreciative to his wife, Andrea, and their three kids, Anna, John, and Laura. Family always comes first.

I've been fortunate to have some of the greatest teachers in the world, Paul Rago, Elizabeth White, Ed Balsdon, Brother Richard Orona, Clinton Bond, Robert Haas, Carol Lashoff, David Alvarez, Giancarlo Trevisan, Bernie Segal, James Frey, Donna Levin, and James Dalessandro.

Thanks to the fantastic friends of my life, John Wible, John Henry, Pete Klenow, Chris Sweeney, Suzanne Golibart, Gina Cioffi Loud, Eric Holm, Susanne Brown, Rick Friedling, Max Swafford, Sherilyn Todd, Rick and Robin Kreutzer, Christie and Joaquim Perreira, and Tricia Mangiapane.

My life has been immensely enriched by the brave whistleblowers I've come across in my writing, such as Judy Mikovits, Frank Ruscetti, Nobel Prize winner, Luc Montagnier, Zach Vorhies, Ryan Hartwig, Mikki Willis, Michael Mazzola, Henry Marx, Cary Poarch, and of course, James O'Keefe, who provides not only a platform, but support for those with the courage to blow the whistle on corruption.

I wish to acknowledge the wonderful staff at Bombardier Books, the brilliant David Bernstein, the amazing Aleigha Kely, and the wonderful Devon Brown. I am honored to serve with all of you in the fight for freedom.

## Cary Poarch

Becca, you were paramount during this whole operation. From being on board (mostly) in the beginning, to picking me up when I was at my lowest. I'll always be grateful for having you by my side during this journey!

Baby Emma, you went from being a thought to actually starting to be created during this venture. The thought of soon having you helped jump my resolve into overdrive. Your mother helped pick me up, and you helped sustain me over the long haul! Team Effort! Daddy loves you, always!

Incredible thanks to James O'Keefe and the whole team at Project Veritas. Having a place to go to share what I was seeing was an indescribable blessing. I obviously couldn't go to the *Washington Post, CBS*, or anywhere else. Thank you for having the vision to make not only my, but all the past and future whistleblower stories happen. You're all heroes of the republic!

Kent, thanks for being the amazing, passionate writer and digger-for-truth that you are. It was a blast working with you and seeing the product develop. In parallel, thanks to Bombardier for green lighting the production. It was great working with you everyone involved!

Randall, thank you for being one of my oldest friends and brothers. You challenged me at multiple points to evaluate my position on things and to start seeing things differently and I'm forever grateful for that and you.

Lucas, thanks for being the friend and brother you are. You have been there through many of my ups and downs. And it was paramount having you there to bounce ideas off of from time to time during this whole journey. Much love!